Customer Satisfaction

Customer Satisfaction

Its Not Just Your Promise Its Your Business

A Walk-Through of Your Small Business from the Customer's Vantage Point to Develop Processes That Guarantee Customer Satisfaction

Chris W. Bryan

ISBN: 978-1-7364298-1-5(Paperback)
ISBN: 978-1-7364298-2-2(E - Book)

Front and back cover design by Anthony Haye – RYSE Design

Customer Satisfaction Services

www.CustomerSatisfactionBook.com
Scan the QR code below for more details

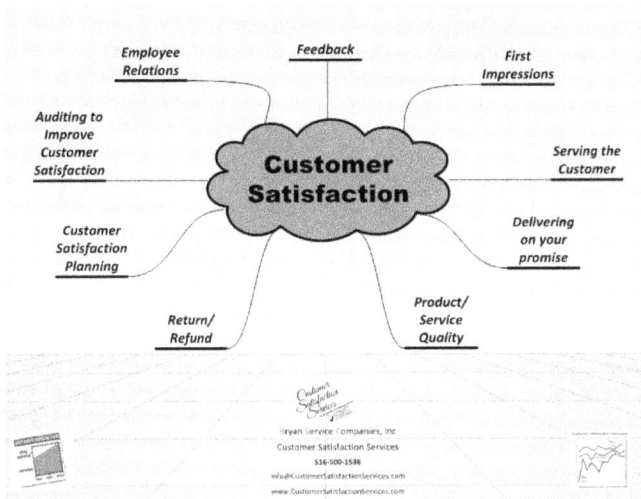

Customer Satisfaction

- Employee Relations
- Feedback
- First Impressions
- Auditing to Improve Customer Satisfaction
- Serving the Customer
- Customer Satisfaction Planning
- Delivering on your promise
- Return/ Refund
- Product/ Service Quality

Bryan Service Companies, Inc
Customer Satisfaction Services
516-500-1586
info@CustomerSatisfactionServices.com
www.CustomerSatisfactionServices.com

BRYAN SERVICES COMPANIES, INC-
CUSTOMERSATISFACTIONSERVICES

CUSTOMER SATISFACTION MINDMAP

Table of Contents

Anyone who thinks customers aren't important should try doing without them for a week.

—Source Unknown

Introduction

What would it take for every single customer that walks through the door to be happy? What things would have to be executed daily to guarantee that each customer walking out the door will come back? Can this happen despite what transpired when they experienced your businesses products, processes, and employees?

This could be the reality for all businesses, but we often get disappointed with the level of Customer Satisfaction received when we approach small businesses in our community for their goods and services. The attitude and level of Customer Satisfaction is often, at the mildest, a "turn-off," and at worst, absolutely atrocious.

This attitude is something that I have encountered enough to inspire me to write this book. This book promises to solve the problem that small business owners face—of not understanding and executing the various elements of a plan for Customer Satisfaction.

So how does a mechanical engineer with a twenty-year career in manufacturing and quality management come to write a book about Customer Satisfaction for small businesses? What would a restaurant, retail shop, spa, or a dry-cleaning business owner get out of this book written by a process and systems thinker? What led to the passion that I have for small businesses and the prospect of building better communities through a focus on Customer Satisfaction for them?

Well, to answer those questions and show how this book can lead to improved small business Customer Satisfaction and business growth, let me take you on a quick trip to Jamaica in the 1980s.

Eager to give their children the best opportunity for an education, Adelsa and R.J. Bryan left the comfort of their homeland in Jamaica and came to the United States and literally started their lives over. Although they had decent jobs in Jamaica, they decided to pack up and leave everything behind and move to New York.

Having been born in Jamaica and migrating to come to the United States is foundational to the story of how I was inspired to develop a passion for the subject of Customer Satisfaction.

The opportunity for education in the United States led me to a high school and college career that was focused on engineering and developing an understanding on how various systems work and come together to produce some of the greatest products in the world.

I migrated to the United States with my parents in the early '80s, where I completed my B.S. in mechanical engineering. I continued my career in manufacturing/quality engineering at one of the world's largest manufacturers of prestige cosmetics, holding several positions managing various quality-assurance groups, gaining vast experience working with manufacturers across the United States, Canada, and Europe to ensure Customer Satisfaction with their products and compliance with global regulations.

My background in management and quality engineering, as well as an entrepreneurial spirit, have led me to develop Bryan Service Companies, Inc—Customer Satisfaction Services, a consulting business that offers a Customer Satisfaction system designed to help small businesses in our communities to understand the impact Customer Satisfaction has to their bottom line, and help them execute on the key principles of guaranteeing Customer Satisfaction and growing their business.

Being a visual person, I had to immerse myself in an environment that would inspire me to write. I became familiar with almost every Starbucks across Long Island, New York, as I would often write and develop my business as I sipped on some iced green tea or a hot medicine ball. Being in that environment inspired me to research and identify the various systems that needed to be in place for someone who wanted to make a claim of being able to guarantee the satisfaction of their customers.

I would often visualize a restaurant and walking through it as a customer, imagining the various interactions I would experience that would impact my choice to return or not. As a result, throughout the book, you will see many examples of how this ideology would be implemented if you owned a restaurant.

A Customer Satisfaction Mind Map was developed to identify the key areas that impacted customer perception and ultimately loyalty. In this book, I outline a step-by-step process for your small business to develop a plan to GUARANTEE Customer Satisfaction and grow revenue. I will walk you through the nine-part framework I have developed that examines each area of a small business's operations that needs a plan developed to control the customer's experiences.

My hope is that anyone can take the general principles outlined and apply it, regardless of the business type, industry, or culture. I may speak about a lot of restaurant stuff, but what I am really talking about is how a business in a retail environment can identify all the physical and digital aspects of their business that impacts the customer experiences. For service-based businesses and those not in a retail environment, I also explore the key elements of Customer Satisfaction that you need to "walk through" in the eyes of the customer.

Being a proud Jamaican and a lover of our food and culture, I would often find myself at a Quick Service Restaurant (QSR) that served Jamaican food. To be fair, I have received less than stellar service from non-Jamaican owned businesses as well, but it would really bother me when a business that was representative of my culture would disappoint me with bad service. I would take it personally because I would see so much potential for the business to grow, and if I was disappointed and not going to return, many others would do the same. The personal connection between Customer Satisfaction, loyalty, and success for small businesses in my community was cemented in my consciousness.

Reading this book will lead to the development and execution of a Customer Satisfaction plan that drives not only an increase in a business's revenues and sustainability but also impacts the people and communities they serve. By implementing the systems and practices discussed in the following chapters, you will have developed a solid Customer Satisfaction plan. With this plan in place and with employees trained, empowered, and having clear expectations, you can expect to guarantee the satisfaction of your customers.

This book does not claim that being able to guarantee to Customer Satisfaction is an easy feat. It doesn't claim that the customer is always right or pretend that 100 percent of the time your customers will be in love with your brand. What it does claim is that if you step back and examine your business from the customer's vantage point, you can identify the issues they will experience in advance and either prevent them from occurring or create processes to acknowledge the issue and win back their favor.

Just in case you are wondering if all this talk about Customer Satisfaction is really worth the investment in time, resources, and money, here are a few facts. Repeat business through

Customer Satisfaction can have a customer lifetime value of ten to one hundred times the original purchase. According to Bain and Company, a 5 percent increase in customer retention produces more than a 25 percent increase in profit. The numbers tell the story and are among the key strategic objectives of some of the world's most profitable companies: Amazon (280.5 billion), Starbucks (26.5 billion), Costco (152.7 billion), and Nordstrom (15.86 billion), to name a few.

As I write this introduction and put the final touches on this book, we are going through one of the most difficult times in history. It has been difficult personally, as many of us have lost loved ones to COVID-19, and it has also been difficult financially as many have lost jobs and businesses. Small businesses play a critical role in the economy as the source of many of the jobs in our community and the tax base to help sustain our neighborhoods. If there ever was a time when we needed small businesses to thrive, it is now! Small business success and longevity is rooted in the ability to consistently provide the citizens of our communities with superior goods, services, and experiences. As we look to rebound small business's ability to not only survive but also thrive, will be contingent upon us all. Small business owners play the obvious role of making Customer Satisfaction not just common sense, but common practice. As consumers, we need to hold the businesses in our communities accountable and provide them with constructive feedback, so they can make the necessary changes to ensure that the level of Customer Satisfaction provided is representative of our communities and culture. As leaders, we need to advocate for small businesses that are serving our communities and partner with them to help build better communities through a focus on Customer Satisfaction.

Businesses, neighborhoods, cities, our country, and the world can thrive through a focus on Customer Satisfaction.

The following chapters serve as a guideline for employers, consumers, and community leaders, detailing the critical components that must be integrated into business in our communities to ensure Customer Satisfaction, repeat customers, and small business longevity.

The first step is to create a great first impression.

One

First Impressions

Customer perception and loyalty are formed upon the first interaction that customers have with your business—whether it is on your website, over the phone, or as they walk through the door. This impression continues to be influenced at every point of contact thereafter with your establishment.

When customers walk into your business for the first time, they immediately begin to form an opinion as to whether they will return. To ensure Customer Satisfaction, you should physically walk through your store and put yourself in the shoes of your customer. This opinion progresses from the moment you open the front door, to the time you wait in line, give your order, use the restroom, and throw out your trash. For most businesses nowadays, the customer experience also includes digital interactions from a Google search to online ordering for pick-up. This "walk-through" is done by looking at each step in your customer's journey as they interact with your business. Try to envision how all these experiences will coalesce in your customer's mind to form an overall opinion of your establishment.

You must design every possible customer interaction with Customer Satisfaction in mind. **As you set up your business—or redesign it—every detail and touchpoint should be analyzed for its customer impact.**

Customer Satisfaction is the overall feeling that a customer associates with your brand due to all aspects of your business that the customer experiences. Customer service is what takes place while performing a transaction for a customer. Customer Satisfaction, on the other hand, is the overall feeling to advocate for your brand or NOT, because of all the experiences that occur during exposure to your brand. Marketing, operations, sales, customer service, product quality, and all other aspects of your business that impact your customer, either directly or indirectly, have an impact on Customer Satisfaction. I make the distinction between the two because, in my opinion, customer service is only a subset of Customer Satisfaction. The Net Promoter Score (NPS) is a standard industry metric for Customer Satisfaction. It is derived from the customer's overall "feeling" about your brand and whether they would ultimately recommend you to a friend or colleague.

My experience has been that most business owners have not taken the time to actually do this exercise of "walking" through their business. In consulting with restaurants and assisting them with this exercise, we have been able to identify many issues that impede the customer experience. We have recommended customer feedback/loyalty programs, onboarding and training programs for new employees, and a methodology for reviewing and responding to online feedback across multiple websites.

LOCATION

When setting up your business, as the old real estate saying goes, the most important thing is location, location, location! The physical location of your establishment is one of the first decisions you make that will have an indelible impact on Customer Satisfaction. Whether your market research is scientifically driven, or based on a gut feeling, it needs to lead to a location that will encourage your customers to return again and again.

Adequate research can lead to identifying locations that may not be booming today, but where you discover that there is a development plan in place that may positively or negatively impact the location. If plans will significantly improve the value of the neighborhood, now is the time to get a foothold into that area, before the commercial rents become unaffordable. Having advance knowledge (prescience) of emerging trends may pay big dividends in the long run. I frequented a bar in Brooklyn that ended up closing. Its location was only a stone's throw away from what is now the Barclay's Center, one of the most highly trafficked areas in Brooklyn. They unfortunately closed about a year before the Barclay's Center was opened. A little prescience about how the area was going to dramatically change in just a couple years may have given the owners more financial incentive to solve the issues that forced them to close.

For a mature business, where your location is already set in stone, you will have to conduct a serious re-evaluation. If your location choice has resulted in serious losses in revenue and poor Customer Satisfaction, then it may be appropriate to consider relocating for long-term success.

If a customer can't find you, or if the location is out of the way or difficult to access, you're off to a bad start! Locations that cannot be easily spotted by pedestrian and street traffic are less convenient for your customers. Another popular saying, "out of sight, out of mind," is relevant here.

Is your business on a main road? Does your customer have to navigate through a maze of streets to get to your location? On what part of the street are you located? These are all questions that new business owners should ask to help identify the optimal location. The corner property in some areas may be the most desirable, but regardless of how your storefront is situated on the block, you must distinguish your business from the others around you.

Ease of access via public transportation is also important, especially if you're in a bustling city where it may be the primary means of transportation for most of your customer base. For your driving customers, an ample amount of available parking is essential. If you plan to be that "happening spot" that everyone goes to, you don't want the amount of available parking to constrain you from maximizing your profits.

Also make sure that your address is highly visible and that you have signage that clearly indicates arrival at your location. Whether you choose for your establishment to be a standalone building, in a plaza, or inside of a mall will greatly depend on the details of your circumstance. Of course, if you are part of a franchise, many of these things will have been predetermined for you.

Additional consideration should be given if the location you are considering has direct access from the outside or is located within a building, such as in a mall. The chosen business model may impact the location, but if the choice is all yours, direct access to the street allows for easier foot traffic and enables customers to locate your store.

As for online businesses, the "location" or ease of finding you online impacts Customer Satisfaction and your revenue as well. Website names that are difficult to spell or that are not intuitive to your business make it harder for desktop and mobile customers to find you. More details about the other factors impacting Customer Satisfaction for online businesses are addressed in Chapter 2, in the section "Website."

LAYOUT

The spatial arrangement of the establishment greatly impacts the "feel" of the place. How does the foot traffic flow through the available space? I encourage you, the owner, to perform a walk-through from the customer's vantage point. This will help identify potential issues that customers may experience. For example, you may be tempted to squeeze one more table in the back of your restaurant, but seating that is too close to the bathroom does not lead to a great experience for the customer, who has to sit there while another customer uses the toilet.

A great overall dining experience for *all* your customers, the repeat business, and the word of mouth that it yields will more than make up for any revenue you "seemingly" lost by not adding that extra table near the restroom. You should also consider acoustics and sound barriers in the restrooms; sounds from the restrooms should not be audible in the dining room.

The entryway to the restaurant should also be open and welcoming and allow for easy access. Many sit-down restaurants have a designated area in the lobby or entryway for customers who are waiting to be seated. I believe this is an excellent opportunity to be as creative as your business model will allow. Use your customers' waiting time to deepen your relationship with them. You can do anything to engage them, from providing a nice atmosphere for the waiting party to personally conversing with them, providing entertainment (be it audio—music or visual or a flat-screen TV). (For additional tips, see the section that follows on "Décor and Theme.")

For quick service restaurants (QSRs), the area where orders are taken usually consists of a basic counter and a path leading up to it, where people wait until they reach the magic moment when it's their turn to order. This is also an opportunity to sell merchandise. In that path leading up to ordering, product displays should be visually appealing, well organized, neat, and full. This can include snacks, bottled drinks, branded merchandise, and gifts. This space and time provides a precious opportunity for you to "WOW" that customer, so he or she will experience the best wait that person ever had in his or her life—and that customer will want to return again and again. Imagine if, while sitting in a crowded waiting area, a few servers came through with sample sizes of the top three items on your menu. Not only does this provide an exceptional wait experience, it can also inspire impulse buys of the items sampled—which can lead to an even bigger order.

Customers are usually curious about the look of the food production area and don't often get to see more than the swinging door that flies back and forth when servers rush out to deliver orders. You can choose to tastefully hide customers from the gory visual details of your kitchen and back office operations. Alternatively, you might dazzle them with the artistry and precision with which you take their order and turn it into a culinary masterpiece by installing an "open kitchen." Anthony's Coal Fired Pizza invites their guests (customers) to be involved in the character and creativity that usually happens behind the scenes by opening up the space and eliminating the walls to the kitchen. A lot of thought should be put into "culinary theater." It is popular with breweries, sushi bars, artisan pizzerias, and many other concepts, as it provides entertainment and social media content. When done right, theatrics can make a lasting impression, while giving your social media engagement and word-of-mouth advertising a boost. On the other hand, if the kitchen is not designed well, or the staff not trained well, it can have the opposite effect. The choice is yours!

Whatever you choose, the pathway for delivering food to customers must have enough room for servers to maneuver, and for customers to get in and out of their seats. Seating the next party of five should not require disturbing a prior party of six that are still enjoying their dining experience.

For takeout establishments, once a customer has placed an order, he or she should have ample space to wait comfortably, without having to practically sit on the laps of the other waiting customers in order to have a seat! Fast food restaurants like Wendy's often leave little space for such a wait, while an establishment like Starbucks maneuvers waiting customers to the other side of the coffee pick-up counter, where they can wait more comfortably.

All restaurants have spaces that are "behind the scenes," such as trash storage, food storage, receiving area, and office space. These areas should intentionally be designed for efficient workflow, while being invisible and unobtrusive to customers.

While you are still in the design stage, make sure your architectural firm of choice has a clear understanding of your concept and vision, and that they incorporate these customer-centric aspects into the layout. Carefully review the drawings of your future or current establishment with an eye for spotting potential inconveniences for your customers, or aspects of your operations that would best be hidden from them. Choose an architect with experience in designing restaurants. They will have knowledge of workflow, building and health codes specific to restaurants, and design elements to maximize the customer experience.

Plan for being very busy. Ask yourself how the quantity and location of the seating, the service stations (where things like napkins and condiments are located), as well as placement of things like the bar or the bathrooms impact the customer experience. Customers who patronize your establishment during the height of your busiest period should not suffer the wrath of angry employees, other impatient customers, or have to deal with hassles like an empty toilet paper roll or overflowing garbage. If cost is a factor, then consider implementing a plan to scale up with an increased number of employees for coverage and service as you get busier. The customers you have during your busiest period should not suffer or experience anything less than your best service. After all, it's thanks to them that you are even busy!

DÉCOR AND THEME

What is the décor? What is the image or theme you are trying to present? Your chosen theme will act as a guide for your décor. Bear in mind that whatever your theme will be judged for its consistency, and anything that doesn't fit into that theme is distracting. This all stems from your menu. The menu determines the branding. Branding starts with the logo.

The graphic designer will determine the brand colors. The interior designer will take those brand colors, logo, and the concept to design the interior. Design should be factored into your start-up costs. Panera Bread and Starbucks do an excellent job in creating a relaxed, welcoming coffee-shop vibe that makes you want to stay, keep buying mocha lattes while you're there, and come back often. Your personal style, creativity, culinary expertise, and cultural influences will greatly impact the décor you select. The key here is to make sure that you are authentic to your theme—while simultaneously keeping your customers in mind.

Appeal to as many of your customers' senses as possible, in order to capture their attention. I visited Reggae Central in North Carolina and was hit with the sweet smell of incense and the sound of Bob Marley & the Wailers' "Rastaman Vibration" playing in the background. As I walked around the store, there were colorful displays of the red, gold, and green colors associated with Rastafarianism. There was no mistaking what the store was all about. It's easy to get this wrong when you have no design skills. Hire someone to do it right.

The objective for you, as a business owner, is to create an experience for your customer that transforms them from the routine activity of eating to a feeling that they are participating in an event created just for them. The décor you choose can actually transcend the time and location your customers are in and take them anywhere you can dream up—even if only for their lunch hour. Utilize this opportunity to create great experiences that will leave your customers wanting to return your establishment repeatedly.

Employee Appearance

Develop a dress policy by establishing what attire and appearance is appropriate and what is inappropriate. Uniforms can be an excellent way for you to establish a dress code and to reinforce your marketing message. They should, of course, fit in with your theme and decor. If aprons or uniforms are required and are supplied by the company, then an adequate quantity should be clean and available. Front-of-house (FOH) staff can be issued branded shirts and should be expected to show up to work in a clean uniform. Employees really should not be taking their aprons home to launder. It is the employer's responsibility to ensure that a cleaning program is in place that sufficiently meets their requirements. It is typical that aprons or chef coats are provided as part of the uniform and there are laundering services who will pick up and deliver aprons.

The physical appearance of your employees has a direct correlation to Customer Satisfaction. Customers will be attracted to your brand if the physical appearance of the employee matches with the brand image. The way that employees dress will help to further cement customers' affinity with your brand. A bank looking to portray a high level of service and professionalism establishes a suit and tie dress code. In contrast, imagine walking into a Chuck E Cheese gaming restaurant for kids, and seeing Chuckie and all the employees dressed in three-piece suits. This correlation between employee appearance and customers' affinity for a brand has been widely studied. In a Johnson & Wales University, MBA student scholarship paper in 2017, "PHYSICAL APPEARANCE IN RETAIL SERVICE: Impact on Customer Loyalty and Experience," it points out that, *"Employees' physical appearance is important in the sense that employees or staff also represent specific characters of the organizations, communicating the brand image and behaving as a kind of 'living signboard.'"* In addition to matching the brand image, the employee should also be well-groomed. Remember that you are serving people food. If food is not handled appropriately, it can make people sick. When a server's appearance is messy, that can translate to "contaminated."

CLEANLINESS

You must plan for the regular upkeep of the facility, especially in areas where customers have access. The food may be great and the service impeccable, but if a trip to the bathroom makes you want to lose your lunch . . . well, that defeats the purpose, doesn't it? A messy bathroom will quickly downgrade a customer's opinion about a restaurant, regardless of how good the food is. Posting a log of the times that the restrooms have been cleaned on the back of the door demonstrates to customers that cleanliness of the facility is a controlled part of your business.

Cleaning of bathrooms should not encroach upon or inconvenience your customers. For instance, closing the restroom during service hours will not go over well with your patrons. I also find it unnecessary for establishments to post that the restrooms are for customers only. I believe this sends the wrong message (it is not customer-centric) and would not encourage me to visit the restaurant at another time.

Consider it a service to the community, and just allow people to use the restroom without feeling uncomfortable. Most people appreciate it enough to remember the kind gesture and will want to return.

While cleaning facilities are important, it should be done without the customer noticing. Unfortunately, I have had experiences while dining out where an employee was spraying cleaning fluid onto a table next to me as I ate. I have also experienced employees mopping the floor prior to closing, with myself and other customers in the restaurant. On one occasion, an employee actually pushed the mop under my feet. While employees should be dedicated to completing their assigned tasks, they must be trained that completion of these tasks should never be intrusive to the customer.

BRAND CONSISTENCY

Your marketing strategy should initially engage potential customers via various touchpoints. Your customers' exposure to your brand probably began long before they entered your facility. Using old school media, radio, print, and TV, along with emerging tools of social media, video, and mobile marketing, you have reached out to customers to teach them about your brand. They have already developed an opinion of what your brand is all about and have come to experience it firsthand. Make sure the brand identity is kept consistent from one store to the next. McDonald's is excellent at this concept, as their menu, design, and layout—even when there are slight variations—are recognizable as part of the McDonald's brand from store to store.

Imagine how confusing it would be to customers who hear about you on the radio and go to your website to find out more information, and discover that the details they see on the site don't match what they have heard. They will immediately start to lose faith in the message that you were trying to send out about how wonderful your establishment is. If you are lucky enough for them to make the effort to take the next step and come into the venue, then the photos they see on your business's website should match what they'll encounter at your actual establishment. This will lead them to feel a sense of familiarity, and further solidify their trust in you as the owner, trust in your business, and trust in your brand.

The Shea Moisture brand experienced this phenomenon as they executed a marketing campaign to grow their business. The brand has traditionally served women of African descent with hair care products that allow them to express themselves through wearing their hair in a variety of ways. As the hair care industry leader serving Black women, Shea has continued to experience massive growth, and the industry has seen many major brands enter this field, which resulted in a bitter fight for market share. Shea Moisture had seen declines in their market share when they attempted to expand by broadening their product line to include products that would serve white women and other ethnic groups. In a series of ads intended to reach out to women across the spectrum, they had a specific ad, which featured several white women and a woman that looked mixed. Many of Shea Moisture's fans became confused when seeing the ad—that was not representative of the client base that typically buys their products. Many customers felt the ad was insensitive and felt the brand was abandoning their core audience. The point here is not that you can't seek to broaden your customer base to increase market share, but that any marketing campaign you do must be consistent with your brand messaging. It must not alienate your current base of customers and must be carefully crafted to ensure that your intentions are genuine and transparent.

Two

Serving the Customer

*T*he various activities involved around serving the customer should be managed appropriately for its impact on Customer Satisfaction. Interaction with your customers or customer service, is one of the most visible aspects of Customer Satisfaction. I choose to make the distinction between the two, as I feel that while customer service is extremely important, it is only a subset of overall Customer Satisfaction. In this chapter we will discuss the components of serving the customer. **By acknowledging the various interactions management and employees have with customers and identifying the many ways these interactions can go awry, you can set a plan in place.**

CUSTOMER ENGAGEMENT

Each customer sought out your product or service to fulfill a specific need. Engaging the customer gives you or your employees an opportunity to find out that need—or problem—so you can suggest a solution. Doing so does not take a lot of time, but does take a little patience and effort on the part of the employee. Sometimes, we get so caught up in what we have to do that we neglect to really acknowledge and listen to the person right in front of us. New customers will walk away totally satisfied when they feel that you have not only sold them what they asked for, but that you have met their specific, individual need. Be aware that sometimes a customer has a general idea of what he or she needs, but may not realize all the products that your establishment has to offer. If your employees engage with customers to talk to them about their specific needs, they may discover that a customer may benefit more from another one of your products that exactly fits what they need.

Another way to engage customers is to make sure that they are specifically invited to return. This special invitation will help to solidify, in a customers' mind, that this is their place to hang out and that they have to come back.

INITIAL GREETING

Imagine if you walk into a well-kept restaurant with the relaxing sounds of Beres Hammond love songs playing in the background, the smell of jerk chicken in the air, and pictures of beautiful beach scenery, only to be greeted by a loud, unfriendly voice asking, "Whey you want?"[1] This would totally undo the vibe that you have spent resources trying to create.

Whether you choose to use a consistent, scripted greeting or an individualized warm greeting, they should both include a smile and an appropriate amount of eye contact. The chain restaurant, Moe's, actually rings a bell and enthusiastically welcomes each guest that walks through the front door with "Welcome to Moe's." As customers walk into your establishment, they should feel a sense of anticipation about the experience that is to come. The opening greeting that sets the scene should, of course, match your theme and décor. A challenge with quick service is that the customer walks through the door into a line. The employees at the counter should be trained to smile and welcome customers while they are in line, even though it may not yet be their turn. Even just a quick smile and a nod will help minimize the customer's perception of wait time until they are in front of you, ready to order. Of course, that's when you smile and say, "Welcome back!" and give them your full attention.

Employees should be trained in telephone etiquette. The initial few seconds of interaction will set the tone for your customer's experience with your establishment. The recorded greeting should identify what business the caller has reached. It should also leave the caller feeling welcomed, regardless of the reason for the call (whether they are calling for directions or to ask a question). There is nothing wrong with providing employees with a script or guideline for what they should say when they answer the phone. This ensures that your company has a consistent message and that all callers feel warmly engaged, regardless of whose shift it is or the time of day.

❖ ❖ ❖

JERK SPOT STORY

I approached the thick plexiglass and spoke through the hole cut out for people to shout their order through. The employee looked at me as I stepped up to the window. I expected her to politely greet me and ask what I would like to order. Instead, I got a stare. I figured she was now getting ready to speak, so I waited and, instead, she again continued to stare at me. We both continued this for an uncomfortable forty seconds until I was forced to tell her what I wanted. If I had not spoken, we would have still been there trying to send imaginary messages to each other.

❖   ❖   ❖

The customer will not differentiate this rude service from a rogue employee from your brand when judging how they were treated while at your establishment. *Employees need to be taught that their attitude is a part of their uniform.* They need to wear that smile and positive attitude the same way you require them to dress up each day for work. The communication that greeters, order takers, servers, and all others have with each customer (and each other) has the biggest impact on how customers "felt" when they were in your restaurant. Make this part of your employee training, and continue to monitor them and encourage them on this point, to ensure that they interact appropriately with customers.

Beyond the first impression, it is vital to remember that the customers in the store are listening. Employees should keep conversations with customers and other employees on a professional level. I have been witness to employees trashing the store owners within earshot of customers. Communication can be both verbal and nonverbal, so employees should be trained to know how their nonverbal communication may impact the customer. Sighing, shoulder shrugging, and refusal to make eye contact all send the message to the customer that they are a nuisance to that employee. "Attitude" should also be part of the employee's regular evaluation. Employees should be evaluated post training, and at least every six months.

PROBLEM RESOLUTION

In the course of interacting with customers, to discern their needs and provide them with a pleasing solution, it is inevitable that mistakes will occur. This may be due to miscommunication from the employee or the customer. Regardless of the true cause, it may result in failure to deliver the goods or service that the customer expects. This impacts ultimate Customer Satisfaction and, by that point, it is actually irrelevant where the communication breakdown occurred.

In life and business, you will encounter challenges, so prepare for them in advance. Employees should be taught how to handle the various personality types of customers and the kinds of issues that are bound to happen. While customers may simply want the problem solved, they also want the issue handled as quickly as possible. They also prefer that the person with whom the issue originates has the power and understanding to resolve it.

If the issue transpired on the phone, rather than in person, then resolving it should be handled with the same level of care. Employees should not place customers on hold for an extended period of time. If they are unable to quickly resolve the issue, then they should return to the phone and update the customer within a set time period. Savvy customers may go as far as asking for the store manager. Employees should not make it difficult for the customer to communicate directly with the manager, and management should make themselves available to speak with customers. If management is not available at the time, the employee should provide a way for the customer to get in touch with the manager.

WEBSITE

Regardless of the line of business that you are in, a website has become a must have for business owners looking to establish their business's credibility, drive traffic to their physical location, and generate (online) sales.

Your website provides a platform to deliver your brand's message, engage the customer, and provide memorable experiences. Through your site, you have a unique opportunity to educate your customers and act as an information resource. By sharing your expertise in the field that your brand is known for, you become a trusted resource to provide valuable content to your customers. As you know, people do businesses with people and brands that they know, like, and trust. So by becoming a trusted resource, you further cement your relationship with your customers.

Many people will judge the service level of your business based on the experience they first have while visiting your website. One of the things I find particularly annoying is when companies deliberately make it difficult to find their contact information. This feels the same as when you call and get an answering service that makes it hard to speak to a live person.

The website can also be used to capture customer feedback. This resource, which you own, can provide a system to capture customer feedback, giving you an opportunity to respond before the customer decides to use other sites, like Yelp and Google, that you have no control over.

It's worth stating again that the branding on your website should be consistent with your product offering and storefront.

A customer's experience on your website should draw them closer to your brand and should support your offline efforts to grow your business. In the same way that you would walk through a physical location, you should click through your website from the home page all the way to placing an order. The experience for your customer should be seamless. A good web designer can implement an appropriate set of web-based tools and technologies that interact with the customer to maximize Customer Satisfaction and sales. The layout, design, brand consistency, and all other elements previously discussed should be considered in your website design. Make sure that whether the visitor is a first-time web user or an experienced web surfer, they can navigate easily and quickly through your site.

If a customer needs help, then getting assistance should be a simple click away, and not buried in some obscure location on the bottom of the page. For a small business with a website selling a product, you will have customers who inevitably want to return something. This is a decision they have already made and you are not going to retain them any longer by making it difficult. If it is apparent to the customer that you purposefully built a system that requires them to jump through several hoops to speak with a live operator or to cancel a service, that customer (who may have previously been a fan or advocate) can quickly turn into your worst nightmare.

ESTABLISH AN ACCEPTABLE WAIT TIME

No one likes to wait in a line, especially when hungry! Waiting is an inevitable experience that some of your customers will have, so why not plan for it in advance? Decide on what is the maximum acceptable wait time that a customer should experience. In my opinion, staff should immediately acknowledge customers as soon as they enter the door. After reaching the maximum wait time (I suggest ten minutes at the very most), staff should apologize to a customer for the long wait.

A contingency plan will need to be in place for what employees should do when they recognize that an excessive number of customers are waiting. For example, one retailer (JCPenney) had a policy that no cashier's line should have more than three people. If the store was so busy that more than three people were in line, the manager on duty was to be notified.

Sometimes, simply verbally acknowledging a customer that has been waiting will suffice. Sincerely apologizing for the wait, and then doing something about it, will go a long way. An experience I had at a Best Buy demonstrates this point perfectly. I brought in a laptop to be fixed, and there were several people in line. It had been about twenty minutes, and I had not been served. A manager stepped up to the counter, asked for everyone's attention, apologized for the long wait time, asked that we be patient, and assured everyone that they would be getting to us. Everyone in the line patiently waited for another twenty minutes without a single complaint.

APPEARANCE OF EMPLOYEES DURING LONG WAIT TIMES

Employees should not give the appearance that they are annoyed that the store is so busy with customers. Having too many customers is a good problem for any store to have! While this situation is more stressful on the employee, if they are confident that there is a plan in place to address an influx of customers, that will put them at ease.

There should be no extra employees hanging around the establishment, especially when the store is busy. If an extra employee is around during a rush, he or she should be trained to pick up the slack and do something to help, even if it's not in his or her regular job description.

I had an experience at a McDonald's that demonstrated this exact issue. I stopped in needing to do some work while waiting to pick up my children, Alec and Kendall, from an event. I stepped up to the counter and an eager young worker took my order for coffee. After taking my order, he went back to the task he had apparently been assigned—of replenishing the ketchup.

The place was quite busy, and there was no one else available, so I waited for more than five minutes while watching this young man, who was arm's length from the coffee machine, but was keeping himself busy with the ketchup. After about ten minutes, the manager asked him if the customer who had ordered the coffee had received it yet, and if he could just serve it to me. Had this young man been trained to keep the customer in focus and pick up the slack as needed, then I would not have been able to tell this story. Even worse is that I recorded a video (http://bit.ly/WaitingforCoffeeatMikiDees) and posted it on Facebook and have further spread the word about this negative experience.

AVAILABLE ACTIVITIES WHILE WAITING

Having to wait to be served can be frustrating, especially when there is nothing to take your mind off the fact that you're standing in line for ten to twenty minutes. As I previously mentioned, many establishments now have flat screen TVs that can help make the waiting experience more pleasurable. Free Wi-Fi service, video games, or a play area for kids can also enhance the customer experience. A manager coming out from the back and apologizing for the wait while handing out samples from the menu would also go a long way.

PHONE CALLS AND LONG LINES

The manner in which a busy store handles incoming calls has the potential to infuriate waiting customers. A bad phone experience can also turn off potential customers, who may have called multiple times and either got placed on hold for a long time or never had their call answered. For on-site customers, the demeanor of the employee is a critical factor in how a customer perceives a situation. If the associate is polite and handles an issue with speed and grace, then you will maintain that customer. A lackadaisical attitude and frustration directed toward the customer will cause people to get angry, and potentially leave the store. A well-trained associate with an understanding of the boundaries of acceptability will be able to resolve this challenge. Employees should be empowered in advance to offer gift certificates or discounts to customers who are able to return at another time.

If your venue is crowded—or busy on all fronts—which of your customers should take precedence? This is a delicate dance that must be learned. Employees should not keep customers on hold on the phone for more than two minutes without some type of acknowledgment. For the person waiting on the phone, they have no way of knowing—and likely do not care about—how many people have been standing in line. If possible, take a phone number and return the call in a few minutes, after the chaos subsides. Better yet, be proactive. Provide menu and location information on your website, make reservations available online, and ordering for takeout available online. This will help limit the number of incoming phone calls to juggle.

SCHEDULE

Another common, misguided practice that I observe is closing a business early when management is not there. If you have established and posted a schedule that states you close at 10:00 p.m., a customer should be served up until that time. Employees can sometimes go into shutdown mode after a long day and begin their closeout activities as early as two hours prior to closing. Their focus shifts from satisfying these "late" customers to getting the hell out of dodge. This practice has to be addressed by the owner setting the proper expectation with employees. It needs to be clearly communicated to workers that at all times during business hours the primary focus needs to be on the customer. Allowances need to be made for employees to have enough time to conduct support tasks like restocking, cleaning, and paperwork. It is appropriate to knock these out while business is slow, but as customers reappear, these tasks need to be put to the side to focus on the customer.

❖ ❖ ❖

STARBUCKS CLOSING STORY

John and I showed up about thirty minutes before closing time at a Starbucks. As soon as we walked in, we could smell the watered-down bleach solution used to clean tables. There were many tables available, so we chose to sit in a comfortable spot, but noticed that the chairs had been turned up. Thinking it was a mistake, I fixed the chairs in order to sit and enjoy the delicious cups of coffee that we had just purchased. As soon as we got comfortable, someone rushed over and abruptly announced, "You can't sit there." I thought it was a mistake, so I asked for a clarification. The person informed me, "You can't sit there because we are about to close." I responded that there were still about twenty minutes from the closing time posted on the doors. She angrily retorted that they were closing soon so they had to get ready. It is apparent that in the mind of this worker, we, as customers, were preventing her from completing her primary mission at this time of the evening, which was cleaning and closing. Was she told that the place "had to be cleaned" and they "had to close at 9:00 p.m."? If so, I can understand her dilemma. Management must ensure that policies like these don't set the wrong tone, which may ultimately negatively impact Customer Satisfaction. On the other hand, the employee may have taken it upon herself to take the hard position—that I have to leave at the time that it says we close, so any customer activity happening too close to closing time just becomes a nuisance. In either case, it is management's duty to ensure a clear understanding of expectations around closing and employees' attitudes toward the customer during the *hours of operation.*

❖　❖　❖

JCPenney has a very good process for closing, by making announcements starting thirty minutes prior to closing time. The tone of the announcements does not change as closing time approaches, and customers are reminded of the time the store opens the next day. Retail outlets and restaurants differ slightly here, but the same premise should be kept in mind—that abruptly kicking customers out is not in the business's long-term best interest. In a quick service setting, personal touch goes a long way. You may not have a loudspeaker to announce the closing time. Instead, a supervisor can visit each table and kindly let them know when they are closing and ask if they would like anything else to go. In a sit-down restaurant, the closing times tend to be a little greyer. Generally, the server (or bartender) will approach the table for last call and drop the check.

On the other side of the spectrum are stores that open late, with many customers standing at the door. The customers standing at your door as you open have obviously made being there a priority over the many other things they could have been doing. I have seen where an employee on the other side of the doors acts as though there is no one standing there until the exact time they are able to open the door. In cases where customers *arrive early*, and you are unable to open a few seconds or minutes early to accommodate them—perhaps due to a staffing issue—then the staff member should explain this instead of ignoring them!

Note

[1.]Jamaican patois reference.

Three

Delivering on Your Promise

SIMPLICITY OF THE ORDERING SYSTEM

Capturing orders in an accurate and efficient manner is a key point in your interaction with customers. The ordering process is another opportunity to engage and relate with customers. It should happen efficiently, but the customer should also not feel rushed. A rushed order is more likely to lead to the customer picking something that was not for them, and may actually cost your small business in the form of a returned product or a negative customer experience.

A clear and efficient ordering system will aid in the collection of the order. For restaurants, a menu that is well laid out and legible will help customers to quickly decide on what they want. There are numerous resources that are available to help in the layout of a hard-copy menu, and you can make display boards fun and interesting, using engaging information and digital technology. Whether you are capturing a customer's requests for laundry/dry-cleaning when clothes are dropped off or the local hair salon getting a new client who wants the latest hairstyle, the customer's ultimate satisfaction is contingent upon you clearly communicating the various offerings and prices.

A well-designed menu/ordering system should give customers all the possible options, without inundating them with too much information. Whether in printed format at a table, a menu board above the counter, or a self-serve kiosk, the information should be organized in a logical fashion that allows the customers to identify what they want based on taste and mood. To capture the customer's order as efficiently as possible, employees can utilize everything from a simple check sheet to a sophisticated POS (Point of Sale) system that captures the order information along with other customer data.

As technology evolves, the main thing to keep in mind here is that whatever menu presentation or POS system your business employs, it must be user-friendly, to give the customer a clear visual of the product offerings. You can use pictures and even video to display the meal or product's features. Many fast-food giants have already mastered this concept by displaying videos of many of their popular menu items. The best time to employ an effective POS system is in the start-up phase. Outside of the start-up phase, consider implementing a new POS system during a slow time, which for restaurants is typically the first quarter. Evaluate solutions based on cost (including merchant services), reporting, ease of use, and integrations with online ordering, payroll, and bookkeeping systems.

THE CUSTOMER'S MOOD

In addition to the high-tech solutions to aid in helping customers to identify what they want, there are also some time-tested, high-touch methods that work equally well, especially in a restaurant setting. Employees who are knowledgeable about the variety of customer options available should take the opportunity to engage with customers and find out what they are in the mood for. Outside of price and availability, the mood of the customer may be one of the most influential factors in the customer making a decision to select a specific item.

A customer's mood may sound like an intangible factor. However, the truth is that it does have a great impact on your customers' buying habits. If your customers are anything like me, they can find themselves frantically scanning the board or menu to pick an item without taking up too much time. Making them feel comfortable, not rushed, will go a long way toward enhancing the customer's overall experience.

A well-trained employee should be able to recognize and intervene in this dilemma. It can alleviate that customer's anxiety, which will lead to the customer having a more pleasurable experience. By asking customers what they are in the mood for, employees can make suggestions based on their knowledge of your offerings.

ACCURACY OF THE ORDER

It's time to deliver on your promise. You spent a great amount of time and money to create a brand and image to bring the customer to your doorstep. Now that they have ordered based on the expectations that you have set, it's time to deliver!

First, did they get exactly what they *thought* they ordered? This is especially critical at a place like a drive-thru or something ordered online. If the order is incorrect, now the customer has to expend energy, time, and money to return the food. This also kills the anticipation that customers had built up while awaiting receipt of the order.

Regardless of how you capture the customer's order, it is important to reconfirm the order before submitting it to be processed. If the customer receives the wrong order, it is irrelevant if the mistake was made by the customer or the person taking the order. The customer will not be happy when they realize that they got something other than what they believed they ordered. In repeating the customer's order back to them or by displaying their order on a screen, it gives them a chance to confirm that what they ordered will satisfy what they need. For example, a customer may get caught up in the moment and order more or less than what they intended to purchase. If the customer leaves the store and does not discover the error until they reach home, they will be severely disappointed with your store.

We all know the old adage, ". . . under promise and over deliver . . ." Make sure your promise is clearly stated and design your process to ensure that you meet and exceed those expectations every time. The strategy of "repeating" or "confirming" the order before completion can be easily integrated into any POS or online shopping cart.

PRESENTATION

The aesthetics of the product delivered should also not disappoint your customer. The presentation of food in particular is a skill studied by chefs around the world. Customers first assess their food by the way it looks. If a picture was involved in the order, then the food should closely resemble the photo that the customer used to order. Also consider this in your back of the house training. Utilize photos that your line cooks can use as a reference tool for each menu item's presentation.

❖   ❖   ❖

RED LOBSTER STORY

A friend recounted an experience that demonstrated this exact point. While watching TV, she saw a commercial for Red Lobster where they have a bowl of lobster and crab that looked sooooo good, as the huge chunks of lobster and crab were splashed into a healthy serving of HOT butter. As a result, she went there with a friend, excited to taste the sumptuous and BIG pieces of lobster and crab shown on the commercial. When she got there, she saw tiny pieces of crab being served with the dish. She felt so tricked by the small pieces that were served versus what was shown in the commercial. The discrepancy was just too big. She lost respect for them owing to their bait and switch tactic. This isn't right! She spoke to the server, who said that many other people had complained about the same thing. She would have preferred it if they had charged more. She was not happy at all.

That's a one-time customer that will never come back.

❖ ❖ ❖

Consider appealing to every one of your customer's senses. It will give you five unique opportunities to solidify a long-term customer. Taste and presentation obviously influence a customer's affinity for your product. Smell is also an important sense that helps connect them to your product. Texture and sound, however, are two senses that may often be overlooked when it comes to appealing to customers.

When your product is food, it may not be apparent how you could use the sense of sound to amaze customers. Get creative in the development stage of your menu and identify ways in which some items could have a sizzling or crackling sound as it is served to customers. The texture of the food can also captivate customers' interests by making them aware of varying textures of foods like cotton candy, mashed potatoes, and salted pretzels. Creatively infusing texture in your foods will round out your command over your customers' five senses and delight them with a meal that they will never forget.

In order to ensure that your product delivers on its aesthetics, taste, and function, it is important for employees to be very familiar with what each meal should look and taste like. Cooks should know exactly what the ideal version of the meal tastes like, and the recipe should be followed consistently.

When it is a service that your small business provides, you also need to consider how it will "look" to the customer. While the customer won't have a physical product in their hand that they can touch, feel, and look at, they will experience the service provided and there may be many instances, whether online or in-person, where the aesthetics of their experience should be considered. The brand image should be upheld in any documents, signage, or promotional items that are part of the customer experience. Get creative about how many of the senses can be triggered when services are being provided. We are still waiting for the invention of "smellovision" to bring the olfactory experience to the customer ordering online. Until that happens, we can bring products to life by employing the senses we can currently experience—those of sight and sound. We can hear and see the benefits that the service should provide and emphasize this in whatever media is used to bring that service to us. The e-mail, landing page, or the package or box used to deliver the service should attempt to utilize sight and sound to excite the customer at the point of delivery. While we may naturally think that we cannot taste, feel, and touch a service being delivered, I am sure that creative imagination aided by constantly changing technology will make this a reality in the near future.

DELIVERY

When delivering the food to the customer, the server should obviously maintain a neat appearance and display an attitude of excitement that the customer is finally going to get the experience that he or she has been waiting for. The method of food delivery should in no way detract from the product itself. I have had takeout food from one of my favorite restaurants, and the food tasted different, due to the packaging used. In this case, the food had absorbed the flavor of the Styrofoam in which it had been packed. Food delivery is an added benefit for customers who want to enjoy your cuisine, but also want the convenience of having it brought to them. This added value is lost, however, when that food arrives in a less optimal condition than how they would have received it if picked up at the store. A pizza that is cold or delivered upside down is inferior to what the customer would have received at the store. With the growth of the multibillion dollar food delivery industry, there are many options for customers to get food and other goods delivered to their doorstep. Delivery platforms have allowed restaurants to reach a broader audience of customers. While the use of food delivery companies like Grubhub, Uber EATS, Seamless, DoorDash, and others have the benefits stated above, it comes with responsibility for the business to ensure that the order's integrity will not be compromised en route to the customer.

Various delivery options also exist for products ordered online. USPS, FedEx, UPS courier services, and other services provide even more options for customers looking to get your products at their convenience. As these options change over time due to enhancements in technology, it is important for small businesses to continually assess if they have the proper controls in place to ensure that customers receive their products and services in a manner that enhances the customer experience.

While product delivery is relatively simple, the delivery of a service to customers is less tangible and requires thought and creativity to ensure that the same level of anticipation exists as when "unboxing" a service that is received. Services typically are provided around necessities that clients have to get to satisfy a necessity, requirement, or regulatory need. Services typically are not sexy and don't naturally lend themselves to clients eagerly anticipating their completion. As service-based providers develop and deliver services to clients, they need to capitalize on the sense of anticipation that customers have while waiting for their product to be delivered.

How is the service being delivered to the customer? Is it a service being delivered through a physical location, like laundry or cleaning services, OR is it a service delivered virtually and the customer is just notified of completion? An example of this may be an insurance company providing a quote and then issuing a policy after identifying the applicable risks and pricing to provide profit for the company while covering the individual.

For services being delivered, the physical elements need to be considered as well. Whether it is the look of the website, e-mail, or text being used to deliver the service being provided or the building, delivery service, or other means of getting the service to them—all have an impact on the customer's perceived value when they obtain the agreed upon service. The less tangible the service means the more you have to ensure that what they see/experience meets or exceeds their expectations.

The very last stop on the customer journey comes with receipt of their product or service. Being the last impression you get to make on the customer, it is critical that a lot of thought goes into how the customer interacts with your product or service as it is being delivered. As with all the other areas of a small business needing to be controlled via a Customer Satisfaction plan, this is no exception. The details of how the customers experience the delivery of your product or service should be fool proofed and reengineered to identify "what could go wrong" and solutions should be arrived at in advance. Now that they successfully received it, the time has come for them to dive in and use and experience the actual product/service.

Let's talk now about the steps to assure Customer Satisfaction as they use what you have worked so hard to get to them.

Four

Product/Service
Quality

For any small business, product/service quality is a key component of Customer Satisfaction, business longevity, and bottom-line success. **Regardless of the industry, it is important that the variables that could impact the quality of your product/service are controlled, in order to increase the likelihood of true Customer Satisfaction.** The quality of the product or service a company provides speaks to how effectively the tangible benefits purported by the company are being received by the customer. Are the benefits you're claiming to deliver being experienced by your customers? Are they being realized on a consistent basis? These benefits and expectations are set through your marketing claims, product specifications, and industry standards/regulations. With consistent delivery of these benefits to your customers, you develop trust for your brand and confidence in your ability to satisfy their needs when they purchase your product or service. ***Based on your specific industry, these benefits/expectations may change, but the same need remains that your operations have control over the product/service attributes that deliver these benefits.***

PACKAGING

In the restaurant industry, packaging quality is critical to Customer Satisfaction when ordering takeout or delivery. The packaging should keep the food hot or cold and prevent leakage. Fast food chains have designed French fry packaging with side vents and no lids, specifically to keep the fries crispy. The big coffee chains test their hot cups regularly for quality control. In addition to choosing quality packaging, consider putting dressings or sauces in soufflé cups when ordered to-go, or altogether eliminating food that doesn't travel well from your takeout menu.

In addition to taste and texture, there are also liability issues to consider. If piping-hot food breaks through the container and leaks onto a customer's clothes, it could mean a lawsuit for your business. A famous case of this was a $2.9 million settlement by McDonald's to a woman who was scalded by their coffee. The facts show that although the lady accidentally spilled the coffee onto her lap, McDonald's was negligent in responding to numerous complaints of "HOT COFFEE" and had a policy requiring the coffee to be at 180–190 degrees, which if spilled, causes third-degree burns in three to seven seconds. The packaging design, policies around the coffee temperature, and their disregard for the numerous customer complaints received ultimately led to the verdict and the bad publicity.

If possible, make sure that only tested and proven packages are used, and that they meet industry standards—and are decorated to your approval.

Oftentimes, food packaging for takeout orders are not given much thought. It is a huge missed opportunity that can be used for further branding and increasing brand loyalty and Customer Satisfaction. While it is understandable that generic packaging may help you to reduce costs, the use of branded packaging for takeout items may actually have a greater impact on the bottom line. Not only will the person who placed the order see your branding, but others nearby will as well. It is at least worth some due diligence to run the numbers to see if branded packaging makes sense for your business. You can also brand secondary packaging that actually carries the food, as well as tertiary packaging, such as bags and boxes. There is no mistaking the pizza delivery giant Domino's for another pizzeria when the delivery guy drives up in his "Domino's car" and gets out with those prominently decorated pizza boxes and bags to keep them hot.

You and your staff should inspect incoming deliveries of packaging materials (plates, cups, bags, utensils, etc.) to ensure that they meet the level of quality that you expect. Quick documentation of such inspection may actually come in handy in case you identify an issue that has to be addressed with your supplier, or in the extreme case of legal action against you, where you have to show that you have done your best to protect the customer.

For services there should also be a consideration for how it is packaged and the impact it has on Customer Satisfaction.

Packaging of services speaks to the way it is presented to the customer and the way in which customers gain access to that service. You surely have heard the saying, "Perception is reality," and in the case of services, it is truly important that the way in which they are put together, packaged, and presented is in such a way that it meets the expectations of the customer. Service being presented with benefits that are not ultimately fulfilled only leads to a demand for a refund and maybe even a bad review, which have an even bigger impact on lost sales.

CONSISTENCY

It's great to have repeat customers, but as customers get more familiar with your product/service, the more critical and discerning they will be. A customer's favorite dish should taste and look the same every time they order it. The manner in which a service is provided should also be consistent. This is where standards and documented procedures serve the purpose of ensuring that every order delivers to the customer's expectations exactly.

❖   ❖   ❖

TROPICAL SMOOTHIE STORY

During the summer of 2010, the members of my office got into the practice of going to a local smoothie spot for lunch. It became a ritual that we would indulge in every chance we got, especially when the temperature got hot. During one of our trips, three of us went and ordered our usual drinks and took them back to the office. I could not wait to get back to work to taste my "Sunny Day" smoothie, so I did so while still in the car. I noticed that mine was more watery than the consistency I had become used to.

My co-workers tasted theirs and we all agreed that there was definitely a systematic quality issue with this batch of smoothies. I called the store and told the manager about the consistency of our smoothies. He apologized for the problem and promised that the next time I was in the store, I would be able to get a free smoothie.

Within a few days, we were in need of a smoothie fix, so we headed to the smoothie joint. I got to the counter and placed an order for a sandwich and notified the cashier of the manager's promise for a free smoothie. The cashier, who was about eighteen years old, was very dismissive and responded that the manager was not currently there. I asked to speak to whoever was in charge at the time.

After some time, another associate, who was about nineteen years old, stepped from the back and appeared annoyed at my request. He went on to say the manager was not available, so he would not be able to give me the free smoothie. I got so annoyed with the way they handled the situation that I decided to cancel my order, return my frequent customer card, and never return to that store again. The manager did the right thing by offering a free drink to welcome me back and try it again, but they should have followed up by mailing me a coupon that any employee would recognize and be able to process. Asking the customer to remember and reference a manager's promise is a hassle to the customer, the staff, and the other customers waiting in line to order.

❖ ❖ ❖

A part of ensuring consistency in food taste is the controlling of ingredients for each of the items on your menu. All your suppliers should be providing you with the same quality of ingredients during each delivery. Only slight variations should be acceptable. Any such differences should never be enough to alter the outcome of your recipes.

Whether your recipes are "secret" or not, I am sure that your chef or cook has a copy that he or she consistently uses to control the taste and cost of each dish being served. This becomes extremely important for customers who are counting calories and base their decision to get a specific meal on the number of calories that you reported. It also provides consistency and stability in production, even when your chef is unavailable.

Food safety is something else that you should consider in this day and age. No matter what your local health department requirements are, all kitchen employees should be ServSafe Certified. This training ensures that all employees who are handling food do so safely, minimizing the risk of foodborne illness (and a PR nightmare for your business).

A log or record of all your ingredients and the dates received and supplier lot numbers will serve as a record of exactly what goes into each dish that you created. If there is a product recall on one of your ingredients, it will be easy to identify the prepared food that needs to be removed from the operation.

The type of food you will be making will determine the kitchen equipment that you will need. You should validate that the specific equipment that you will be purchasing will be able to produce your specific type of cuisine with consistency, and under the conditions that you will be preparing it. Your team needs to maintain proper calibration of measuring equipment to ensure that temperatures, weights, times, or any other critical aspects of food preparation are measured consistently in order to produce favorable outcomes. Inspect kitchen equipment periodically to ensure that it's in proper working order. Keep a calendar and log of preventive maintenance, especially for equipment that requires inspections.

In order to protect the customer and your reputation from food poisoning, it is important that you have an efficient system for cleaning and sanitizing your kitchen equipment, pots, pans, utensils, and the cooking and storage areas. It is equally important that any utensils, plates, cloth napkins, and other items customers use are thoroughly cleaned. No customer wants to use a napkin with faded stains or a fork with water spots from the dishwasher.

This should go without saying, but regardless of how impeccable your service may be or how incredible your food may taste, you will quickly develop a horrible reputation if an observant customer is able to see a roach emerge from your kitchen. I recall in the movie *Ratatouille*, where the owner, who is also the maître d', shows the most important critic in Paris around the restaurant, showing all the fine cuisine. As he lifts the metal chaffer containing food, to show the latest dish, what emerges from the tray prompts the critic to scream, "RAT!!!!!!" Don't let this be your restaurant.

You should employ a pest control service as a preventive measure. Regular service will prevent pest infestation before it becomes a problem. A good technician will block up holes, set bait and traps, and report back on your facility's cleanliness. You also need a properly trained and adequately staffed kitchen to operate equipment and handle the volume of food you need to produce to keep your customers satisfied.

You can control the pace at which your staff delivers food to waiting customers by having a host. The host is clearly able to clearly see what the kitchen has on its queue of meals to be delivered and the inflow of guests waiting to be seated. A knowledgeable host can strike the balance needed to keep both customers waiting to be seated and customers waiting for their meals happy.

RELIABILITY OF SERVICE

Consistency in the quality of service being delivered is key to developing long-term trust and faith in your brand. Regardless of how you attract customers to your service, it is imperative that a consistent level of service be delivered to sustain a long-term relationship with your customers.

Having hundreds, thousands, or millions of customers land on your site and purchase your service is every entrepreneur's dream. With that happening, you are likely to have sales that meet or exceed your expectations. To have these customers return to buy again in a repeatable daily, monthly, or annual fashion would lead to a predictable income stream. For a small business owner, launching their business like this would be the answer to their prayers. This manifesting into reality is centered around the customer receiving the same superb quality of service on a consistent basis. Not only on the first visit, when you are trying to impress them, but during every visit, the customer should come to expect that each order placed would produce the same effective result and be delivered in the same professional and engaging manner.

Earlier in the chapter, we dove into product quality and utilized a food product example to dive deeper into how to evaluate the various factors that impact the quality of a product. In looking at services, it is often more difficult to describe the elements that make up how quality of services is provided. The biggest distinction between the two is the receipt of a tangible item when a product is being provided. As a result, the customer is likely to judge the quality independently and on its own merits.

The quality of a service provided is often judged with criteria that is more subjective than the clear descriptions used for product quality. Let's look at a life insurance policy as an example. Its purpose is to provide security and peace of mind to policy owners that in the event that they were to pass away, their loved ones would be taken care of and be able to resume life as normally as possible. How would you judge the quality of the policy? Was it delivered on time? Did the service meet its intended purpose? Is the effectiveness of the service comparable to previous receipt(s)?

Five

Return/Refund Policy

Mistakes are inevitable in life and in business. A customer having to return a product is already indicative of a disappointing experience on his or her end. Customers shouldn't also have to endure a cumbersome return process that entails an unreasonable additional amount of time and money. **While having to return a product is a major killer of Customer Satisfaction, what makes it worse is when the process is designed to be difficult on purpose.**

It is important that management establish a policy for the return of products, cancellation of service, and issuance of a refund that is acceptable to the customer.

Before we jump into the logistics of execution of a return policy, let's actually discuss the obstacles that small business owners face in having to deal with returns and the logic behind why a good return policy is a must for small businesses.

For small business owners in the growth phase of their business, cash flow is often an issue that can cripple them, if not managed well. On a monthly and quarterly basis, savvy small businesses will monitor their income and reconcile against their expenses and liabilities to ensure they have the cash available to operate the business. A returned product at a later time period can throw many businesses off, as returns that take from your income and increase liabilities can throw things off. It may seem like preventing returns would solve this issue. The argument for a Customer Satisfaction plan being a part of overall business planning comes into play here.

Customer returns are a natural part of any business. While we aim to eliminate or minimize the return of products/services, it is actually smart to build in an acceptable percentage of returns (based on sales) that is reasonable for your industry into your business planning. Having an expected amount of returns built into your budget will allow for you to create a return policy that will provide comfort to prospective clients and will actually increase sales. Driving down returns through continuous improvements, budgeting for an acceptable level of returns, along with an attractive return policy, will maximize Customer Satisfaction, leading to growth. In contrast, simply having NO return policy or one that leaves potential customers with discomfort toward making a purchase will stifle the growth of the business. If a retailer doesn't give this guarantee, then consumers often become suspicious and avoid buying the product, or won't return. I can speak for two well-known brands that I am a fan of because of their generous return policy. Both Amazon and Costco have a very customer-centric return policy that I have taken advantage of.

After establishing a return policy that works for your small business, it is important that it is communicated to clients in a clear manner. As customers consider purchasing from your business, they should easily be able to review the terms of your return/refund policy. In a restaurant setting, there is typically no clear-cut return policy. However, it is understood that if something isn't to the guest's liking, it is remade correctly, or something else is offered in its place. This policy should be formalized, made available to employees, and provided in the customer service training.

SETTING THE TONE

Your policy will set the tone for what an employee's attitude should be when a customer is returning a product. Remember, just because someone is returning a product, it does not reduce their potential as a repeat customer. The same attitude and care that is extended to a customer upon initial purchase should be extended when that customer returns a product or makes a complaint. Associates who get paid based on commissions should be warned that their disappointment in the loss of a sale should not be apparent to the customer. Rather, it should encourage them to achieve a win-win purchasing situation.

Employees should embrace the fact that a customer having to return a product is an opportunity to recapture the good graces—and maintain the loyalty—of that customer. Product quality is an entire subject unto itself (covered in the previous chapter), and you should implement various processes to ensure that the quality of the product or service that you provide not only meets, but exceeds the customer's expectations. If that fails, it's time to pull out all the stops to make sure that the customer still leaves with a high level of Customer Satisfaction.

As with life, when you make a mistake, the first step needed is a sincere apology. It is almost irrelevant at this point where the source of the error originated. Regardless of whether it was the customer's mistake in ordering, or a misuse of the product, it is important for you to be sincerely apologetic to the customer for missing out on the opportunity to provide him or her with the benefit of the product or service.

As I am sure you've heard before: "People don't care how much you know, until they know how much you care." Once they understand that you care, you can quickly move to the transactional part of the return. Whether you or your employees are engaged in the return process, seek to efficiently capture the original product-purchase details, and keep the tone of the interaction pleasant and appreciative of the opportunity to serve the customer again. These details will become important later on, as you determine the true root cause of the issue and put corrective actions in place to prevent further occurrences.

If a product or service does not perform as expected, encourage customers to return the product or ask for a service refund. This gives them a voice and an opportunity to express their displeasure directly to the company versus taking out their frustration on social media. Only approximately 4 percent of dissatisfied customers let the company know of the problem. The other 96 percent vote with their feet (or with their fingers in a virtual world). The reasons for not complaining are that they either don't know how to register a complaint, don't think it will do any good, feel awkward or pushy, or are afraid the company will fight back.

Employees also need to feel comfortable and empowered when making a decision on what they can do to make a disgruntled customer happy. This is not the time to conduct an interrogation that forces the customer to defend him or herself. This line of questioning will make customers wonder why they bothered to purchase the product in the first place, or perhaps that they should not bother to return the product in question and just never come back.

SIMPLICITY/EASE OF THE RETURN PROCESS

The ease of returns should encourage customer participation in the process. This is also a good opportunity to collect data that can aid in analysis of the complaint, but it should not be intrusive, time-consuming, or painful for the customer. If a rewards program is in place, it may be appropriate to award points to customers with complaints.

At this time, it should be left to the customer's discretion to determine if he or she wants an exchange or a full refund. Regardless of the customer's ultimate choice, you still have to recover from the lapse in Customer Satisfaction that transpired during the original purchase. To at least break even, you will have to invest in this customer to bring the level of Customer Satisfaction back to where it was when that customer first entered your establishment. Think of it this way: The marketing dollars you would have to invest to recover from the customer complaint iceberg effect (see: http://bit.ly/CustomerComplaintIceberg) created by this one dissatisfied customer is well worth the investment in a bonus offer to that customer. The iceberg effect is explained below.

❖   ❖   ❖

A COMPLAINT FROM ONE CUSTOMER IS JUST THE TIP OF THE ICEBERG!
For every single complaint made there are about twenty-five people with the same issue who made no formal complaint.

You now have twenty-six UNSATISFIED CUSTOMERS who will typically tell ten people about their bad experience.

That's now 260 people who have heard about someone else's bad experience with your brand. These people will typically tell five people, which results in over 1,300 people who have a negative impression about your brand.

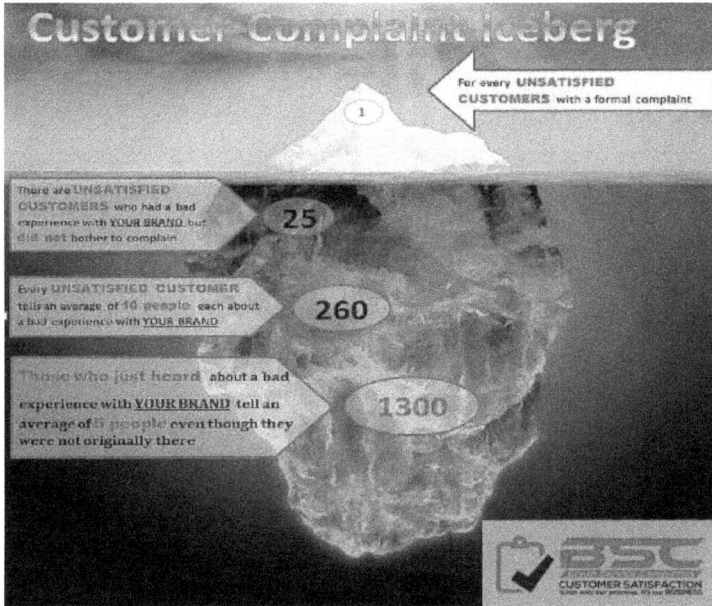

Address each complaint no matter how small, get to the root cause, and implement a corrective action.

❖   ❖   ❖

In a dining situation, a refund is usually not the best course of action. If the guest doesn't like the dish, they are likely still hungry and therefore, perhaps irritated. In this situation, remove the offending item immediately and replace it with another meal that the customer agrees is a good alternative, as quickly as possible. You may also want to comp the guest a free drink or dessert to show your appreciation for bringing the issue to your attention (and increase the likelihood of them coming back and telling their friends and family they had a positive experience).

So, make that investment now, and put your money where your mouth is in regard to how much you value Customer Satisfaction. The spirit in which you deliver this offer should be one of humility. You are wooing the customer to give your business a chance to get it right this time by providing him or her with an awesome customer experience through a value proposition that far exceeds their original purchase.

AVAILABILITY OF MANAGEMENT

Customers will often ask to speak to management if they feel they are not getting satisfactory responses during a complaint. A management representative should be available in order to diffuse the situation or resolve the customer's concern. While visiting a Starbucks, I noticed that the store's managers had business cards available on a placard that encouraged customers to contact them with any feedback. Similar contact information for management should be easily accessible to the customers without them having to ask a frustrated associate. "Can I speak to the manager/owner?" is a question asked very often by customers seeking to resolve issues or ask questions. It is not practical for the manager/owner to be available for every customer request. It is, however, a good idea to have a presence at scheduled times during operations. "Management by Walking Around" accomplishes many objectives and has great benefits. PepsiCo and Starbucks have been a huge proponent of this management philosophy. By having a physical presence, you can better empathize with the day-to-day challenges that your team encounters and therefore build greater rapport and increase loyalty. Being able to interact with customers and address their concerns in real time also has a benefit to customers in getting solutions in a timelier manner versus hearing, "Let me check with my manager" and waiting for what seems like an eternity for the employee to return. Leading by example, you are also able to demonstrate to employees the proper way to interact with clients and resolve issues. Seeing the boss actually do what she has been telling you to do for years goes a long way in building employee morale.

MINE FOR THE GOLD IN YOUR COMPLAINTS

There is no better opportunity to provide customer service than when you receive a customer complaint. Market research and focus groups can be money well spent, but don't overlook the fact that you have direct—free—data as to what is important to your customers—through their complaints. You should formally capture what makes your patrons unhappy, then use it to improve your processes. An analysis of a complaint can uncover the root cause of the problem and several other types of causes that can lead to this same issue. If you correct these potential causes, then you can benefit from the customer complaint.

The exact numbers may vary slightly among many experts on Customer Satisfaction, but I recommend that you should survey upwards of 50 percent of your customer base once or twice every year. Put a well-managed program in place to reach out to your customer base on a regular basis, so that you can assess what their interaction with your team has been like.

Utilizing this feedback from customers to drive innovation and improvement will ultimately lead to less complaints and the need for a returned product or cancelled service around those specific issues.

Six

Customer Satisfaction Planning

As I've demonstrated throughout this book, having a greater percentage of satisfied customers does not happen by accident—but with careful thought, planning, and execution of an overall Customer Satisfaction plan. Ideally, this should be documented and woven into your business plan and procedures, so you and your staff can consistently execute it.

MISSION STATEMENT

You can quickly tell if a company has high regard for its customers' satisfaction by reading its mission statement. This may be the first interaction that a customer (or potential investor) has with your company, and it tells how much value you place on the customer—if at all.

The mission statement sets the tone for how you will implement staffing, training, processes, and procedures, in order to carry out the mission. Good examples of well-crafted mission statements vary widely, but all accomplish the identification of a company's core purpose.

Culver's restaurants, with over 428 restaurants in nineteen states throughout the Midwest have a very simple mission statement: *Every guest who chooses Culver's leaves happy.* On the other hand, a company like Maxie's Supper Club and Oyster Bar in Ithaca spent time to develop a mission statement that addresses every area of their operation. Their mission statement reads:

> *Our goal is to: sell delicious and remarkable food and drinks. That the food and drink we sell meets the highest standards of quality, freshness and seasonality and combines both modern-creative and traditional southern styles of cooking. To consistently provide our customers with impeccable service by demonstrating warmth, graciousness, efficiency, knowledge, professionalism and integrity in our work. To have every customer who comes through our doors leave impressed by Maxie's and excited to come back again. To create and maintain a restaurant that is comprehensive and exceptional in its attention to every detail of operation. To provide all who work with us a friendly, cooperative and rewarding environment which encourages long-term, satisfying, growth employment. To keep our concept fresh, exciting and on the cutting edge of the hospitality and entertainment industry. To be*

a giving member of the Ithaca community and to use our restaurant to improve the quality of life in the Finger Lakes region.

While I have not yet visited either of these restaurants, by looking at their websites, it is my opinion that they have clearly defined their mission and have a very high regard for the satisfaction of their customers. Each company has likely developed a systematic approach to achieve Customer Satisfaction. Each of these approaches to planning for Customer Satisfaction may be as unique as each company's mission statement. A Customer Satisfaction consultation looking at the nine key areas outlined in this book and evaluation of their operations would confirm if they have accurately executed them to achieve their mission.

The current focus on Customer Satisfaction has evolved out of the old quality-assurance approach. Companies used to focus only on the specific product or service to ensure it met certain specifications that they believed were important to the customer. Customer Satisfaction focuses on the customer's experience with the product, and their perception of the quality of the product based on their interaction with it.

ANTICIPATE CUSTOMERS' NEEDS IN ADVANCE

Understanding your customers' needs and being able to execute a streamlined process will make their experience more enjoyable. Many of the interactions that occur daily with customers are predictable. ***Your Customer Satisfaction plan should address how to handle the majority of potential issues that will occur. By taking the time to capture all these potential issues, and then identifying all possible causes, you can develop solutions to prevent them, and then train employees on how to seamlessly address most of the issues that may occur.***

TRAINING

Training in Customer Satisfaction techniques is important and will provide a standard against which employees can judge their skills. You should use both general and industry-specific Customer Satisfaction training to develop your training curriculum. It can be customized to meet the specific needs of customers in your industry, market, or local culture.

Employees' intimate knowledge of the products and services they're providing is critical to exceptional customer experience. If an employee knows all the features and options in a product, then he or she is able to genuinely help to solve a customer's "problem." That customer has a need that has to be satisfied, and that is what he or she should get help in resolving.

If a customer is hungry and looking for something quick to eat, or on a date and looking for a chance to enjoy a meal with someone special, those are two very different scenarios that demand a different focus to satisfy that customer's needs. An inattentive waiter may suggest or provide an experience that will turn that customer into a detractor, instead of an advocate.

On numerous occasions, I have been to a restaurant and needed quick service, due to an impending meeting. A request to the waiter for fast service spells out my primary need in *this* specific circumstance. All the other aspects of the customer experience that are laid out in this book are still important to me on a personal level, but fast service is a *must*, in order for me to be satisfied. Employees are often so wrapped up in *their* job that they are not observant of what's going on around them.

❖ ❖ ❖

THE TAXI DRIVER

An experience I had with a taxi driver demonstrates how being alert, observant, and not self-absorbed leads to great customer experiences. It was your typical clear New York fall day, and I needed to get to work after dropping off my car to get fixed. I decided to take public transportation and asked a cab driver what the price would be to get to my destination. His response almost made me fall off my chair. I declined the ride and started to think of alternative means to get to work. Another cab driver who was in earshot overheard the conversation and volunteered a solution for me: "You can take a cab to the Babylon train station and then take the N72 bus to route 110 and then transfer to the S1 bus." The cost would be dramatically less, and I had the time, so I jumped in his cab. Thanks to him, I got to where I needed to go. This was because he was knowledgeable about his route and was observant of what was going on around him.

Small business owners and employees alike can learn a great lesson from this cab driver—that to provide Customer Satisfaction you must get out of your own head about your "job" and observe what the needs are of the people around you. This example sets apart the "order taker" from the customer service professional. It's not just about fulfilling an order; it's about finding a solution that best fits the customer's needs. It is this win-win solution that leads to Customer Satisfaction, repeat business, and growth. When you integrate this idea into your customer service training, it gets your staff more comfortable with the idea of "selling." Selling should never be dishonest. It should be helpful, courteous, and have the ultimate goal of Customer Satisfaction.

❖   ❖   ❖

REMINDERS

As you develop a plan to satisfy your customers, you should consider providing reminders to your staff and customers. Posters and banners can be useful tools in training activities. They can also help to remind your employees of their role in ensuring that customers' needs and expectations are met as they get immersed in the business of doing their job. Providing reminders to your team on a regular basis helps to reinforce your commitment to the satisfaction of your customers. Technology should be utilized where possible to provide this same inspiration for employees to remain customer-centric. There are numerous sources of great content on customer service that can be provided to employees at low or no cost. Many managers and owners with this mind for customer service will encourage their teams to subscribe to blogs and newsletters that promote great customer service. By enrolling, the employees are acquiring knowledge that will be helpful for life.

Signage is also a way to convey to customers what management's expectations are about your establishment's customer service practices and policies. Your mission statement, return policy, management contact information, and other important information can be communicated to your customers using printed or electronic media. This sets the tone for how employees will interact and also improves the customer's confidence level in your commitment to overall Customer Satisfaction.

INCENTIVES: SHOW ME THE MONEY

If you value Customer Satisfaction, then put your money where your mouth is! The best way to demonstrate to your employees and customers that Customer Satisfaction is important to your business is to reward employees that meet and exceed your established standard. This does not necessarily have to be a cash reward, but it should definitely have significant value to your employees. It's your preference whether you choose, for instance, to give movie tickets, days off, or gift cards.

Many people would think that compensation is the most important factor that impacts employee relations and, therefore, Customer Satisfaction. I would argue that it is a factor, but not the most important one. What is important about compensation is that you offer employees a fair and competitive wage. Even more important is that you recognize their efforts to improve their performance. You can also tie employee compensation to Customer Satisfaction in order to reinforce it as a priority. This goes beyond their tips for a job well done.

Your direct base compensation to your employees can include a bonus-based incentive that encourages employees to deliver the kind of service that receives positive customer feedback. By tying Customer Satisfaction to bonus compensation, you are showing how important this is to your bottom line—so important that you are willing to invest in it. Employees that do not meet your minimum standard need to receive feedback as well, and the appropriate disciplinary action taken. That disciplinary action could include warnings, probation, and eventually termination. We recommend conducting semiannual evaluations that cover the following areas: customer service; reliability, availability and punctuality; attitude, drive, and initiative; knowledge and communication; technical skills; and cleanliness and work habits.

CUSTOMER LOYALTY

There are numerous studies on customer loyalty and its impact on a company's bottom line. The three main components of customer loyalty are retention, advocacy, and purchasing.

Surveys of customers can provide valuable insight into a customer's willingness to remain and recommend your product to other people, as well as the likelihood of that customer purchasing new products.[1]

If you do lose a customer, then you lose your opportunity to offer additional products or services. The real value of your business is in your base of repeat customers. This is where residual oncome comes into play. Having a customer continually purchase your product or service over time—when you initially acquired them weeks, months, or years ago—is one of the building blocks to true wealth. When you have a significant number of customers that have now become fans of your brand, you can actually bank on this future income. For example, in the coffee world, the value of a customer is roughly $8,000 over their lifetime. The customer lifetime sales value is $13k for a pizza operator. The cost of comping a latte or pizza is miniscule compared to the lifetime value if you can gain that customer's loyalty. The lifetime for a family restaurant in a stable community would be much longer. One grocery store chain figures that the lifetime for one of its customer is ten years, so let's use that. The lifetime value of a guest who spends $12 with you three times a week is $18,720. And that's just from one guest. Keep a family of four happy—mother, father, and two kids—and that lifetime value jumps to $74,880.

Loyal customers can eventually turn into raving fans that advocate for your brand. These ambassadors amount to free advertising, which definitely has a significant dollar value. Word of mouth is the oldest form of advertising, and it is absolutely free. Customers that love your products, adore the service provided, and connect with your over-all mission can become advocates and fans that go the extra mile to make sure that the people they know have a chance to share in the same experience that they have had. Check out the "Red Napkin Tip" by Jon Taffer on Gary Vaynerchucks blog-podcast: https://www.garyvaynerchuk.com/three-best-restaurant-tips-customer-retention/

WILLINGNESS TO RETURN AND SHOP AGAIN

The third component of customer loyalty is your customers' willingness to continue to patronize your establishment and spend their hard-earned money. Loyal customers can account for a significant portion of your revenue. This is what makes an investment in executing your Customer Satisfaction plan extremely lucrative. The return on investment in this area is as significant as investments in advertising, research and development, infrastructure, or operations.

Note:

[1] QP magazine–March 2011, "Customer Loyalty: The Right Mix of Measures," p. 24.

Seven

Inspect What You Expect

S mall business owners need to be aware of what is required, not only to satisfy their customers, but to comply with the requirements of regulatory bodies whose job is to protect consumers.

The viability of a Customer Satisfaction plan requires a small business to establish the expectation of superb customer service and the metrics to measure it. Having this expectation ingrained into the culture increases the likelihood of a successful internal or external audit.

Consumer protection and safety is the primary concern of regulators that enact laws. While Customer Satisfaction is not their concern, it is the ultimate objective of regulators to pass laws that protect consumers and ensure that they are not dissatisfied with products that cause harm or pose a risk to the health and safety of the public. The reputation of your brand is directly linked to your public image and consumer trust that you will continually deliver products and services that meet the scrutiny of regulators.

To know if your operation is meeting the requirements of regulatory bodies, local regulations, or policies and procedures established by your company, an internal audit performed by a manager can be very helpful. The issue with this is that the manager is often too close to what is going on to remain completely objective. You don't want to wait for the regulatory body in charge of your industry (e.g., FDA, EPA, OSHA, or the Department of Health) to show up, in order to determine how you are truly doing. By then it would be too late.

The link between Customer Satisfaction and conducting audits of your business is as follows. To ingrain the expectation of excellence in Customer Satisfaction into your staff they must feel the carrot and the stick. The carrot is all the forward thinking, training, and programs you put in place to raise awareness of Customer Satisfaction. The stick is that natural fear that motivates employees to be on their best behavior, because they understand that you have a system in place to observe their activities around Customer Satisfaction. There are consequences for their actions, good and bad.

The concept of "trust but verify" should be employed here, to ensure that all of the best-laid plans and significant expenses that you have invested in your business are being carried out to your expectation. By simply setting the expectation that there is a possibility of a surprise audit, you can encourage employees to be on their best behavior. *Inspecting what you expect simply establishes that you regard the satisfaction of your customers to be extremely important, and that you are willing to spend the time and resources to ensure that management and employees are executing your expectations as planned.*

COMPLIANCE WITH REGULATORY REQUIREMENTS

It is the responsibility of ownership to ensure awareness and to take steps to comply with relevant laws, policies, and regulations. In fact, it is the ownership that is legally responsible for compliance and be held personally liable if a business does not fully comply to protect its customers.

An independent organization that is familiar in the proper auditing techniques of your industry can help your operation to identify gaps in your procedures and find areas that do not comply with regulatory requirements. An audit's purpose is to identify areas that need improvement. It can be painful to hear someone else be critical of something that you've put your blood, sweat, and tears into, but it is absolutely necessary, so you can proactively address potentially critical issues.

There are many industry trade association groups that advocate for small businesses. These associations can be a great resource in identifying the specific regulatory bodies that preside over your industry and have jurisdiction over the area within which your small business resides. It is important to become very familiar with the actual regulations that are in place to protect your customers. For example, in July of 2018, the FDA imposed a regulation on QSRs with more than twenty locations—that they must implement a method of communicating caloric content and nutritional facts to their customers. Awareness of this new requirement within reasonable timing is key, in order to digest if it would be applicable to your establishment, and to identify cost-effective solutions to ensure compliance.

You would not want to inadvertently violate a local law simply because you are not aware of it. Ignorance is not bliss! You are still held accountable if you are unaware that a practice that you employ in your small business violates local, state, or national laws that govern your industry. In the restaurant business, the local Department of Health typically has such jurisdiction over food-handling practices. On top of industry-specific issues, there are also labor law issues that vary by municipality, like minimum wage or paid sick leave.

As a new small business owner, it is prudent to ensure you are clear on regulatory requirements of your industry before making significant investments into your new venture. As stated previously, the selection of your location impacts your customer, but it also should be considered for the potential environmental impact and the resulting regulatory requirements based on the site chosen. Extensive research should be done based on the services and goods you intend to provide to customers. Each industry comes with its own local, state, and federal agency and ensuing laws, restrictions, registration fees, and fines—all established to protect the consumer.

An objective eye, taking a serious look at the regular practices that exist within your small business, can be a huge asset in the long run. A mock audit simulates an audit done by a regulatory agency, but is conducted by an internal resource or outsourced. It is important to treat these mock audits with the utmost seriousness, so you can get a true indication of what would happen if a real inspector shows up at your door. If you take this approach seriously and investigate any issues you've identified, then the audit would have been money well spent. Doing an audit like this may uncover some issues that require an investment. Better to know that ahead time, as a fine or closure is typically much worse—the opportunity cost of being closed, on top of the PR nightmare that can result, whether that's not complying with new labor laws or a food safety issue that compromises trust in your brand.

SECRET SHOPPING

Secret shopping is another tool to inspect what you expect. A secret shopper can give an eye-opening look at what real customers experience whenever they enter your place of business. A secret shopper can capture the true picture of what happens during your absence and provide you with a verbal, written, or video report. You can use the insights you gain from this firsthand information to give you a clear understanding of how your employees handle your customers. This can help with making operational improvements, and with staff evaluations and incentives.

I like to capture occurrences on video. It gives you the opportunity to show your employees exactly how they conduct themselves in front of customers. I believe that constructive feedback goes much further than a public beating, but if the incident warranted action being taken against the employee, then you have captured irrefutable evidence. In addition, you can use the footage to put together employee-training initiatives. You may actually catch them doing something great, and can use the video for positive feedback and examples of Customer Satisfaction. Footage of employees demonstrating exemplary customer service may also be incorporated into your marketing and training materials. I have to add here that you need to have employees agree to this in advance, during the hiring stage, and also ensure that you don't inadvertently violate any local or state laws around capturing video.

Along these same lines, you can also use your security cameras that are deployed in strategic locations within your establishment. The amazing thing is that even though people initially know that they are being monitored on video, they quickly become comfortable and forget that the cameras are in use. They revert to their natural practices, and you will have an ongoing monitoring system to check how employees are executing Customer Satisfaction.

Ensuring compliance requires you to be proactive and organized. Meeting the expectations set by regulatory guidelines does take some time and attention that is outside of the day-to-day operations and focus on profitability. It is tied to profitability, but because many companies have to go bankrupt due to lack of compliance, and because of the high cost of overcoming the high fines caused by multiple violations.

The compliance landscape is always evolving, and your responsibilities grow as you expand.

Eight

Employee Relations

The way you treat your staff sets the tone for the way they interact with your customers. Disgruntled employees who feel slighted and berated are not who you want to have interacting with your customers.

INTERNAL CUSTOMERS

Employees are your internal customers, and their satisfaction is based on the fulfillment of basic human needs of respect, fairness, and a feeling of support, through resources and training. A simple smile radiating from one of your employees can have an invaluable impact on your customers. Employees who bring the challenges of their personal lives to work and wear them on their faces have a negative impact on your business. Take the time to genuinely inquire about how they're doing—both in and outside of work—and empathize with them, while letting them know that everyone goes through challenges. When it comes time to work, then the smile is a part of their uniform and must be worn.

This approach should be taken by the management of every small business to improve morale in the workplace. At first glance, it might appear that employee morale is not the responsibility of the business owner. It may be thought that employees should be responsible enough for their own personal and mental well-being and show up for work prepared to interact with customers. As a new business owner or manager, you may not think this is your responsibility. This is about leadership. Lead by example, lead by walking around, lead by empathy. This is proven to work, and the sooner you realize it, the better off your business will be.

Empirical analysis has shown that not only are the actions of employees fundamental for a high-quality delivery of service but also that their morale influences consumer satisfaction.[1]

Yes, employees should be responsible adults, showing up and being ready to work. It is also important, though, that employers are aware that the more they foster a culture that supports and builds on the self-esteem and morale of their employees, the more positive impact they will have on how those employees treat their customers.

In early 1994, Continental Airlines was among the worst airlines to travel on and had horrible Customer Satisfaction metrics to prove it. For years, Continental had been teetering on the brink of bankruptcy, and relations between the CEO and workforce were quite contentious. Customers experienced this toxic environment through severely delayed flights and lost baggage.

In a *Harvard Business Review* article titled, "Right Away and All at Once: How We Saved Continental" (September–October 1998 issue) by Greg Brenneman, the then president and CEO of Continental, writes, "Continental ranked tenth out of the ten largest U.S. airlines in all key customer service areas as measured by the Department of Transportation: on-time arrivals, baggage handling, customer complaints, and involuntary denied boardings."

In February 1994, they brought in a new COO, Gordon Bethune, who was later promoted when the CEO had had enough and resigned. Charged with turning the company around and rescuing them from certain bankruptcy, he turned his attention to employee morale as one of the first areas that needed to be fixed.

Gordon Bethune was quoted in a *Forbes* article, "Management Advice from The CEO Who Saved Continental Airlines": "Your employees and their attitudes are the differentiating competitive edge you have, and I think we utilized that extensively while I was at Continental. You have to gain and earn the trust of your employees. But not only that, you have to make them feel rewarded in order to get your product at a level that it can beat the competition . . ."

Bethune started with changes to how employees could interact with corporate executives by opening the doors to the executive suite. A new open-door policy was instituted to allow employees to express concerns and provide input. This change in culture did not go over well with many of the top executives, who were subsequently fired. Bethune got out onto the front-lines and visited pilots, airline mechanics, baggage handlers, and stewardesses. He implemented weekly communication with the Continental workers to educate them on his vision to turn the company around. Employees also had the opportunity to respond directly back to the CEO through voicemails. This openness and transparency about the company's plan laid the foundation for all the changes that resulted in Continental's turnaround. During Gordon Bethune's tenure, Continental went on to earn the most coveted symbol of excellence in Customer Satisfaction—the JD Power & Associates awards.

TWO-PRONGED APPROACH

The employee or the customer? Who comes first in your attempts to improve on Customer Satisfaction? Where do you focus your efforts to improve the satisfaction of your customers? Do you create systems and programs geared at making your customers feel more attracted to your brand through superb customer experiences? Or, do you focus internally on your employees to enhance the environment in which they work to enable them to emanate the positive vibes that you would like your customers to experience? It depends.

Achieving your ultimate goal of increased Customer Satisfaction happens by development of a Customer Satisfaction plan as outlined in this book. While many of the systems and processes critical to your plan are customer focused, this chapter delves into the employee focused activities that enhance Customer Satisfaction. Ideally, as you establish your new business and develop your business/ Customer Satisfaction plan, you should be designing these employee engagement practices into your operation. Before you open the doors to collect a dime from your first customer, your employees should have experienced the environment and culture that will eventually attract your customers to become lifelong fans.

> **Your employees are your company's real competitive advantage. They're the ones making the magic happen—so long as their needs are being met.**
>
> —Sir Richard Branson

The needs of your employees are quite basic. They are looking for a safe environment to work where they can fulfill their financial obligations—a place where they feel appreciated for work that they feel is meaningful. Meeting these basic needs of employees leads to a fully engaged workforce, where their full talents and attention are fully realized.

A 2017 study by IBM's Smarter Workforce Institute and the Work human Analytics and Research Institute, titled "The Financial Impact of a Positive Employee Experience," sought to understand the optimal working experience for employees and how perceptions of the relationship with their employer impacted their work performance. In setting up the study, an Employee Experience Index was established, which measured the core aspects of employee experience. These are listed below and can serve as tangible things that employers can evaluate to quantify the level of engagement of their workers:

- Belonging–feeling part of a team, group, or organization.
- Purpose–understanding why one's work matters.
- Achievement–a sense of accomplishment in the work that is done.
- Happiness–the pleasant feeling arising in and around work.
- Vigor–the presence of energy, enthusiasm, and excitement at work.

Through evaluation of the employee experience—with over 23,000 survey participants from forty-five countries—they concluded that "more positive employee experiences are linked to better performance, extra effort at work, and lower turnover intentions." Employees working on this higher level of morale and feeling more in tune with their own values and the values of the company are more likely to interact with your customers in a positive manner.

WHO ARE YOU HIRING??

One of the first steps in executing your Customer Satisfaction plan is the hiring of employees who fit into the culture of your business and are able to execute your plans. By starting out with hiring the right employees, you put yourself miles ahead of the game in creating an environment where customers will be satisfied. Zappos is recognized as an industry leader, not for shoes, but for superb customer service. Their former CEO, Tony Hsieh, was very outspoken about the role that hiring "the right people" has in creating a culture that breeds great customer service. In a 2010 article printed in the *Harvard Business Review*, Hsieh explained, "Would you expect someone who wasn't happy at work to exude and embrace those values on the phone? With the right hiring practices and company culture, you don't need to spend millions on training: Our hope was that if we get the culture right most of the other stuff will just happen naturally on its own."

Some of the key characteristics to identify when hiring employees who will be successful in customer service include emotional intelligence, communication skills, resourcefulness, and passion. In addition, your application process should screen for availability, scheduling gaps, long-term employment potential, and attitude.

Zappos spends an incredible amount of energy on their hiring practices and on the rare occasion when they get it wrong and hire a "misfit" for their culture, they encourage that person to leave by presenting "the offer" of a $2,000 bonus for them to quit after their first week. While this may not be a fit for small businesses, I do think it makes the point of the importance of hiring the right people from a company that is world renowned for customer service and trains hundreds of other companies on the art of customer service.

SET THE TONE (TRAINING)

The way that you treat your employees and the policies which you have in place to manage your greatest asset (your staff), both have a direct impact on your customers and their feelings toward your brand. The principles that you apply to your employees will be mirrored by them when they interact with your customers.

As mentioned before, owners and managers set the tone for Customer Satisfaction by prescribing the expected etiquette employees should use toward customers. This should be clearly spelled out in the documented training system you have in place. Ideally, provide employees with real-life examples and scenarios where your staff members employ the level of customer service you expect.

Your employees are the most visible component of your Customer Satisfaction plan, so it is well worth the investment to ensure that they are properly trained to execute on your plan to satisfy your customers. Costs vary greatly and depend on the medium chosen to deliver the training. There are many generic training programs that you can buy off the shelf, but there are great benefits to consulting with an expert who can design a program that is specific to your industry, location, and culture.

Online training/webinars can be a convenient lower cost method to deliver Customer Satisfaction training. Individual workers can gain easy access to the information during a convenient time. Costs can range from as low as $30 to $80 per person, or more, depending on the chosen provider.

Software for generic customer training programs can also provide another low-cost solution and can enable you to present the information to as many individuals as possible without any additional cost. There is a lot of merit to conducting the training in a group setting, where employees can interact with management and share current scenarios with fellow classmates. With costs as low as $80, software can go up to $1,000 for more specialized training.

There is also a lot of value in making the investment to bring in an outside consultant who can offer the latest techniques in customer service training. Both management and employees can benefit greatly from an understanding of what competitors and other industries are doing to train employees on customer service. Bringing a fresh outside voice that is unbiased and knowledgeable about the general topic of customer service provides tremendous value. At the top of the food chain is Zappos' school of WoW Customer Service training where they share insights on the customer service culture they developed, which eventually attracted Amazon to buy them for $940 million.

In deciding what route to take for executing customer service training, the upfront cost per employee has to be weighed against the potential impact to revenue. Once you have established the budget, you can determine the content.

WHAT SHOULD TRAINING ON CUSTOMER SERVICE ENTAIL?

There are some basic principles about customer service that management and staff should be trained on. As mentioned, employee welfare is at the center of providing superb customer service, so any training program on customer service must inspire your employees to show up as their best self. The need for personal and professional development needs to be introduced to employees so they gain a thirst for continuous improvement and continually upgrading their skills.

Another critical skill will be how to interact with customers. It cannot be taken for granted that employees know how to communicate with customers. They will be the face of the company and are usually the primary component of Customer Satisfaction that customers complain about. Being able to discuss any question, issue, or concern that a customer has will be a core skill. See Chapter 2—Serving the Customer—and the section on "Engagement with the Customer."

Product knowledge is an extremely valuable component for employees dealing in customer service. While it could be conducted as separate to the customer service training itself, it has to eventually become a vital aspect of training. The key to employees being able to show empathy toward customers is for them to have experience and knowledge of your products. Whether it is having favorites or just understanding how the product has benefited them or another customer, it will go a long way.

It is important for the employee to have an understanding of the ground rules or policies by which the company has to abide. Whether it is company policy or industry regulations, the frontline employees dealing with customers need to have awareness. I would caution employers, however, not to hide behind policies as excuses to justify inability to deliver on cus-tomer service. In the event that delivering on the customer's needs results in a gross violation of policy, then an alternate solution should be sought.

BUILD TRANSFERABLE SKILLS

It is critical for employees to buy into the concept of Customer Satisfaction and to see how it is in their direct interest to hold your customers in high regard. After all, it is customer business that keeps them employed. *By providing your employees with the interpersonal skills and tools you weave into your training program, you are giving them transferable skills that will be with them for the rest of their lives.* If employ-ees can understand the impact that Customer Satisfaction has on your bottom line and their continued employment, it can help show them why they should have a vested interest in delivering outstanding service. This becomes an asset that they have that no one can take away from them. *Those inter-personal skills and the ability to relate to customers can go a long way in helping them to find their next job, or even to start their own businesses.*

ENVIRONMENT

As the owner of the small business, it is your responsibility to ensure that the environment of your facility does not have a negative impact on both your employees and customers. Basic conditions such as the temperature, air quality, acoustics, and lighting should be designed for the comfort of employees who will be in the space for a prolonged period of time. The satisfaction of your staff is linked to their work output and the satisfaction of your customers. As a result, the physical conditions under which your staff work is a direct impact on Customer Satisfaction. The various components of Indoor Environmental Quality have requirements that are mandated by local, state, and federal agencies like the EPA, OSHA, and ASHRAE. It is important to be aware of these requirements and get the appropriate professional help to ensure they are being met.

It is also your responsibility, as the small business owner, to protect employees from customers who may become verbally or physically abusive. Make the employee understand that you "have their back" if a situation should get out of hand. By doing so, they will get a sense of comfort, knowing that they don't need to take on a defensive posture with a customer. Assure them that management will handle any situation that escalates above a certain level.

By ensuring that these needs are met, you are helping to ensure that your employees feel physically and emotionally safe and secure, and prepared to interact with your customers at ease and with a smile.

Note:
1. *http://docplayer.net/35719606-Organisational-effectiveness-and-customer-satisfaction.html*

Nine

Customer Feedback

Many small businesses fail to provide any significant level of Customer Satisfaction because they have not made it important to get feedback on how they are doing. Ignoring customer feedback is probably the simplest to overcome of the "Top-5 Killers of Customer Satisfaction."

Measurement and feedback on Customer Satisfaction is extremely important for employees, management, and the company in general.

Let's begin by ensuring that all interested parties clearly understand what customer feedback is exactly. Business dictionary.com defines it as:

Information coming directly from customers about the satisfaction or dissatisfaction they feel with a product or a service. Customer comments and complaints given to a company are an important resource for improving and addressing the needs and wants of the customer.

It is important that employees and small business owners focus on the second sentence in the definition, where it claims feedback as a resource for making improvements. Feedback comes in both in formal and informal ways, but must both be captured and addressed to gain their benefits.

Informal feedback may be given directly to staff or ownership during the customer experience. Well-trained employees should be encouraged and equipped to capture this informal feedback. Developing a culture that encourages feedback goes a long way. Informal feedback may be verbal, as a customer expresses their gratitude for an employee assisting them. A complaint voiced to an employee or management has equally important value, or maybe even more important than a compliment from a happy customer. It may also be nonverbal, as a well-trained employee is able to identify that a customer is not at all happy with the service being provided. No matter if it is negative or positive, informal feedback is important to capture. Doing so requires ownership to lay a strong foundation as to its importance and getting creative with the simple mechanisms that will be used to capture it. Capturing informal feedback can consist of jotting down the basics as soon as possible after the event occurred.

Formal feedback comes through the various mechanisms that you have set up in advance. Awareness of these various feedback mechanisms should be second nature to your employees. It is again important that both positive and negative feedback be encouraged to be captured, utilizing your formal feedback systems. Employees should be able to articulate the value the company sees in receiving feedback and be able to encourage customers to utilize the most convenient mechanism to capture it. Employees should be able to encourage and direct them to any formal feedback system you have set up—whether it's going to your website, calling the phone number on the back of the receipt, or clicking on a feedback message and link visible on their phone. Technology can be a great tool to make the capturing of formal feedback fun, simple, and effective. It is important to capture data on a regular basis, not just when a customer is upset about something. Look for common themes in the feedback to make operational improvements. Keep the customer comment card short and sweet. Use it for marketing purposes, promoting social handles, and asking for e-mail addresses and contact info for your newsletter, but keep the feedback portion simple with questions like: *What did you like the most? What could we do better*? Again, you'll find those common themes.

Surveys are a form of customer feedback that are often ignored. Surveying of customers can be very valuable in capturing the data to understand the industry-wide metric used to measure Customer Satisfaction. The Net Promoter Score (NPS) is often used to understand how willing customers would be to advocate for your small business and refer you to their friends or colleagues. By asking this question during surveys, you will be able to calculate your business's NPS. This score will enable you to compare how you measure up to your competitors and other industries. Although businesses have only been measuring Customer Satisfaction using the NPS since 2003, the concept of Customer Satisfaction has existed since we began trading goods and services.

In one of the first customer complaints recorded in 1750 B.C., an ancient Babylonian consumer takes a considerable amount of time to carve his complaint onto a clay tablet. *"I will not accept here any copper from you that is not of fine quality. I shall (from now on) select and take the ingots individually in my own yard, and I shall exercise against you my right of rejection because you have treated me with contempt . . ."*[1]

Could you imagine the amount of time it took to carve each of the words captured in the original 293-word complaint? I can imagine the anger and disgust with which this angry customer chipped away at the hard slate tablet to ensure that the merchant got the message that he was displeased with the quality of the ingots provided for his hard-earned money. While the medium to provide customer feedback has gotten significantly easier over the last 3,000 years, the same emotions may well exist in your customers today.

The only way that you will know how much impact Customer Satisfaction and its improvement have on your bottom line is by measuring them. Capturing this information will enable you to understand what is truly important to your customer, so you can provide more of it. Oftentimes, we assume that we know what the customer wants, but actively end up developing a product or service based on our own interests and desires. Gaining feedback from your customer base will truly tell you how profitable and sustainable your business model is—and inspire viable new products, services, and concepts to improve and innovate your business.

While some customers willingly give feedback, a great majority of customers do not take the time to express their satisfaction or displeasure with your brand. In either case, I believe it is important to gather this data. It is the responsibility of the small business to make the process of capturing customer feedback as smooth as possible. Various factors impact customers' willingness to provide feedback. Firstly, the media used to capture the feedback must be simple and allow for the customer to easily be "heard." In addition, customers must feel comfortable and not have to "fight" with employees or management to provide their feedback. There are some cultural aspects to this as well, as feedback is perceived by some as snitching or not being in support of the business if feedback is provided to management, especially when it is a complaint.

I have experienced that Japanese customers are very knowledgeable about the products they buy. They politely demand answers as to how the products became defective and are interested in what corrective actions will be taken to address the circumstances under which the product became defective. Therefore, it is important for the staff to understand how customer complaints are fielded and ultimately addressed in the operation.

Regardless of the impact of culture on providing feedback, it is important for small businesses to embrace and encourage all forms of feedback.

For the consumer that is interested in the gains that customer feedback can bring, it is important to provide that feedback so that the information can ultimately be used to make improvements that benefit the community. **The greatest impact that the community can have on an existing small business is to give customer feedback. By giving**

both positive and negative feedback, the small business is able to address the concerns or give the community more of what it is asking for. An engaged community providing feedback to small businesses will tend to lead to businesses striving to provide better goods and services and ultimately more profitable and sustainable businesses.

These potential benefits of customer feedback come from stepping back and taking a look at the various touchpoints where you and your staff interact with customers. Giving your customers an opportunity to evaluate your company's performance will tell you how to effectively improve in deficient areas. Technology provides so many ways for us to seamlessly obtain this information. Whether you choose to capture this information at the point of sale, or shortly thereafter, you can easily do so with today's technology.

As previously mentioned, your customers are already giving feedback, so they are already measuring your performance. Through apps like Facebook, Yelp, and Google Reviews, to name a few, your customers are already grading you on Customer Satisfaction and announcing it to the world. Be proactive and measure your customer's degree of satisfaction yourself.

You can ensure that the metrics are properly defined, and reflect what is important to all customers that you serve. You have no control, however, over the feedback provided by your customers who are using social media and other customer-feedback apps. The first step in managing your brand's Customer Satisfaction image is to be aware. By monitoring your online customer feedback (on a wide range of platforms), you can get an overall sense of how you are doing.

By looking at as many sites as possible, you get a very clear picture across all the important customer demographics that support your small business. Analysis of the details from this feedback can be a gem for making improvements to your business that will go straight to the bottom line.

If you are doing anything worthwhile, then people are talking about you, so you don't have to look very far to capture feedback from your customers. Having an effective social media presence and keeping up with the latest breaking news has become extremely important to remain connected with your customers. When this breaking news is about your product, service, company, or industry, it is even more important that a plan that was well thought out in advance gets executed to handle the situation. An effective social media plan will encompass "listening," so that when your business is mentioned online—whether through news or a customer comment—you are alerted.

Having a dedicated person who is in tune with what's being said about you online is key. With awareness, you can now take action to address and fix the bad press and embrace and promote any good coverage. Having knowledge of your company's reviews on vital feedback sites is the first step. The best way to combat a number of bad reviews is to fight back with good ones. In other words, it's a numbers game. I would also recommend addressing the bad ones though, which is an acquired skill. A public response can go a long way, as most customers are more interested in how you respond, than in the original complaint.

That said, when responding to a negative comment thank the customer for the opportunity to address the issue.

Your business should encourage customers who had a positive experience with your product or service to go to these sites and provide a review. Do not be tempted to fight bad online reviews by getting them erased, or by getting people to put up fake reviews for you. People can spot this a mile away, and it can permanently sink your brand if you are exposed to be padding online reviews of your company with pay-for-play submissions. You can, however, execute a campaign to have all your satisfied customers go to the prominent online review sites and provide honest feedback.

By accurately collecting this data, you now have "golden nuggets" of information that you can use to enhance your current product line and develop brand-new products to meet your customers' needs. By continually applying the repeat cycle of "Plan, Do, Check, Act," you can have a never-ending stream of new and improved products that specifically satisfy the needs of your customer. This concept of "Plan, Do, Check Act" is a simple project management tool used across various industries to verify that you are addressing problems with viable solutions. By continually coming up with an effective plan to address the issue, executing that plan, measuring its effectiveness, and then following through based on its effectiveness, you will continually improve the situation and eventually implement a permanent solution.

By really listening to the voices of your customers and identifying a true solution to the issues they raise, you now are in tune with what your customers really want—if enough of them voice the same desires and concerns, you also know that they are willing to pay to get it. By proactively following up on this information—and doing so with notable solutions—you have now cemented your relationships with those particular customers for life.

There are numerous ways to receive customer feedback, which you can use to improve your operations. In-store complaints, phone calls, and letters should be treated seriously, and your staff should resolve issues to the customer's satisfaction. You can obtain customer feedback via print media or telephone or online surveys. Social media websites like Facebook, Twitter, Yelp, and many others have increased opportunities for customers to provide feedback. You can also use customer receipts or aspects of your packaging to direct them to use a phone number, website, or text message in order to give their feedback, positive or negative. You can incentivize customers to participate in such feedback mechanisms by offering them a coupon or store discount. Delivering a Customer Comment Card with the check and an incentive to win a gift card will help round out the feedback you receive to a good sample size for accurate data collection.

It is important for employees to be aware of the metrics that the company uses to determine a Customer Satisfaction rating. Create a storyboard, mount it on the wall, along with feedback from customers, so associates will be able to see how their efforts impact the customer experience. JCPenney did an excellent job of this as part its overall plan to perform superior customer service. Associates actually crowd around the board to read the customers comments, and it creates a sense of pride and stirs friendly competition. You can incorporate reviews into the staff meeting agenda—good and bad. Have the staff break up into groups to draft a response to bad review as practice in handling a disgruntled customer. Read through the responses and correct any that missed the mark and discuss why.

You also need to obtain customer feedback in a timely and efficient manner. Having the details and being able to react within hours or a day—as opposed to weeks or months—is much more useful to the customer and to your business. The focus of the feedback process should be on identifying a solution, versus punishment of a specific individual. If employees understand this, then they will be more cooperative and volunteer critical information. Complaints can be a second chance to keep a customer's business—if changes are made based on the feedback.

Note:

[1]   http://www.openculture.com/2015/03/the-first-recorded-customer-service-complaint-from-1750-b-c.html

Ten

Building Better Communities through Customer Satisfaction

We have spent the previous nine chapters focusing on Customer Satisfaction, and how a small business owner can zoom in on each of the main points in these nine chapters, in order to identify opportunities to put systems and practices in place that ensure Customer Satisfaction.

As you bring all these points together into a Customer Satisfaction plan for your small business, they become a blueprint that you can build into company practices, policies, and culture, after which you train employees on and hold them accountable. Once these activities and systems are now at the fingertips of the soldiers that your company has on the frontline of the company-customer experience, let them know that you expect them to consistently deploy these best practices they've been formally trained in, so no ambiguity exists on their expected behavior.

It is at this point that Customer Satisfaction becomes controllable to you, as the small business owner. It is then that small business owners could consider opening another location and duplicating the same system of controls. It is also at this point that we have begun to build better communities through Customer Satisfaction.

The knowledge and confidence such formalized training provides to employees not only impacts the bottom line, but also has a spillover effect onto the community which the small business serves. Such knowledge and confidence are rooted in the skills that employees acquire through the training that you provide them with as a small business owner, in your quest for Customer Satisfaction.

These transferable skills can be redeployed by the employee as they continue into the workforce at another job, or as they start their own business. A community with more "customer-centric" employees and small business owners can uplift the spirits of customers and local community members through the superior products and services that they provide.

This cycle continues, as customers are encouraged to spend their hard-earned dollars within their community. In turn, such business vibrancy helps to attract additional new businesses and residents to that neighborhood. The cycle further continues, as residents demand that other businesses uphold these standards through superb experiences, an expectation of superior customer service, and a focus on Customer

Satisfaction. It's through such **education** and **expectations** that we are able to **Build Better Communities through Customer Satisfaction.**

❖ ❖ ❖

CUSTOMER SATISFACTION SERVICES

❖ ❖ ❖

This book was written as a first step in the process to empower small businesses to GUARANTEE the satisfaction of their customers—leading to continued business growth and longevity.

Small business's failure due to lack of a sustainable source of customers is a problem worth solving. It comes from a lack of repeat business, referrals, and natural business growth, and not paying attention to the key elements of Customer Satisfaction executed though a well thought out CUSTOMER SATISFACTION PLAN.

Bryan Service Companies, Inc—Customer Satisfaction Services helps Small Businesses Educate, Evaluate, and Execute on the critical strategies to guarantee Customer

Satisfaction and grow your business. This is accomplished through the articles, books, surveys, courses, and consultations we put out.

❖ ❖ ❖

Sign up for a complimentary 30-minute consultation @
https://www.customersatisfactionservices.com/customer-satisfaction-consultation-FREE_30mins
You can also join our community, the Facebook group: "Building Better Communities Through Customer Satisfaction" Facebook Group: https://www.facebook.com/groups/BBCTCS/

Chris can be contacted directly for speaking engagements, consultations, and networking at:
e-mail: info@CustomerSatisfactionServices.com
You can get more information at the following websites:
https://www.customersatisfactionservices.com
https://www.bit.ly/CustomerSatisfactionServices

Follow us on social media at the sites below:
Instagram: https://www.instagram.com/Customer_Satisfaction_Services/
Facebook: https://www.facebook.com/Customer SatisfactionServices
YouTube: http://bit.ly/CustomerSatisfactionServices_YouTubeChannel
LinkedIn: https://www.linkedin.com/company/customer-satisfaction-services

Please scan QR code on back cover to connect to the above sites and get current information.

Acknowledgements

While this book is about the subject of Customer Satisfaction, the impetus for writing it has had everything to do with my life over the last seven years. As such, I must start with my incredible parents, Adelsa and R.J., who were courageous enough to leave our beautiful homeland of Jamaica and venture to America to start over with the hope of providing their kids and future generations with opportunities for education and prosperity. The values that they imparted to us, both consciously and subliminally, have led to educational and entrepreneurial pursuits. My own journey into entrepreneurship has been a winding road, taking me along numerous paths lined with people who have had a significant impact on the direction of that entrepreneurial travel and its twists and turns.

While there are numerous people to thank, I must limit it to those instrumental to this book coming to fruition. After having two beautiful kids, Alec and Kendall, my marriage ended, and I was in search of answers to ensure that

I identified my true gifts and talents, and utilized them to ensure personal satisfaction for myself and financial stability for my kids.

In the spring of 2011, I was introduced to Ms. Bobbie Hicks through a colleague who recommended her as a potential business coach. That first meeting at a lower Manhattan hotel lobby ended up changing the trajectory that I would head down. Bobbie helped to stir up my creativity and inspired me to identify that the frustration that I had been feeling in observing the lack of focus on Customer Satisfaction in Jamaican-owned businesses was a larger problem, and a message that only I could tell in my own words—based on my culture, educational and professional backgrounds, and entrepreneurial experiences.

Discovering your calling is one thing. Writing this book and building a successful business to address the concerns identified in that calling is a whole other thing—and probably the hardest thing I have done in my life.

Yet another angel that has flown alongside me as I have trotted down this difficult path is my girlfriend, Jackie. I cannot express how grateful I am to her for her belief, support, and patience during this entire process. While there are a few others that I could spend another couple of pages thanking, I will leave the final acknowledgments to the family, friends, colleagues, and coaches who have helped inspire me to connect the dots and solidify my mission for *Building Better Communities through Customer Satisfaction.*

About the Author

Chris Bryan was born in Kingston, Jamaica. He attended Marlimount Primary (Old Harbour, St. Catherine) and Campion College (i.e., the equivalent of middle school), before migrating to the United States in 1982. He continued his education at Frank D. Whalen J.H.S. in the Bronx and then went on to Brooklyn Tech High School, where he graduated in 1987.

Upon graduation, he attended Cornell University, where he began his studies for an engineering degree. After encountering some financial challenges, Chris left Cornell and completed his degree in mechanical engineering studies at Rochester Institute of Technology, where he received his B.S. in mechanical engineering.

Chris was recruited by General Electric ("GE") to join their Manufacturing Management Program (MMP), and took on assignments in both Cleveland, Ohio, and Albany, New York. It was while on assignment in Cleveland at GE's Tungsten Products Plant that Chris first learned the concepts and principles of quality engineering, and obtained his Six Sigma Green Belt

Certification. Many of the principles, concepts, tools, and problem-solving techniques that he learned during that time have become the foundation upon which Chris has built his career in manufacturing, quality engineering, and quality management.

Chris continued his career in manufacturing/quality engineering at one of the largest manufacturers in the world of prestige beauty products, holding several positions and managing various quality-assurance groups. He then went to work with the Supplier Quality Assurance team. It was here that Chris gained vast experience in working with factories across the United States, Canada, and Europe to ensure compliance with federal regulations for the manufacture of cosmetics and over-the-counter drugs.

Chris' background in engineering, management, and quality engineering, and his entrepreneurial spirit led him to develop a consulting business, where he provides clients with processes, products, and services that improve Customer Satisfaction and increase revenues.

His personal mission—"Building Better Communities through Customer Satisfaction"—was the impetus for developing his consulting business—Customer Satisfaction Services. When given an opportunity to address audiences via speeches, workshops, and panels, Chris often encourages small business owners to "inspect what you expect," and professionals in corporate America to "build transferable skills."

Chris finds it particularly disturbing when he sees Jamaican-owned businesses gain a poor reputation for Customer Satisfaction. One of his personal goals is to help raise the level of Customer Satisfaction that is expected from Jamaican-owned businesses.

He holds certifications from the American Society of Quality (ASQ) including Certified Quality Manager/Operational Excellence (CQM/OE–ASQ), and Certified Quality Auditor (CQA–ASQ). In addition, he is a Certified Six Sigma Green Belt (GE) and Certified Packaging Professional (CPP).

Chris currently resides in Long Island, New York, where he enjoys the great outdoors, riding his bicycle and spending time with his children (Alec and Kendall) and his girlfriend Jackie.

CONTACT INFORMATION

Website:
https://www.bit.ly/CustomerSatisfactionServices
www.CustomerSatisfactionServices.com

E-mail: info@CustomerSatisfactionServices.com